About the author

Blair Stevenson helps contact centre leaders create and sustain a world-class coaching culture, so they boost employee engagement and drive results. He's specialised in this work for 25 years. If there is such a thing as a "super-power", then this is his.

Blair is the CEO of BravaTrak – the coaching system for contact centres.

He created this system based on the findings from more than 83 years of behavioural science research, has refined it with over 12,700 managers, and has helped clients generate more than $107 million in cost savings and sales revenue. Blair has spent more than $4.79 million on perfecting it.

He guarantees his clients will increase performance by at least 11% in 6 months, or they get their money back. Many increase performance by more than 21% within a year.

Those clients have included contact centres and retail networks across more than 53 large organisations serving more than 17 industries.

Blair holds a Bachelor of Arts degree in Psychology and a Diploma in Teaching. He lives in Auckland, New Zealand, with his wife Gill and enjoys recreational road cycling and competitive rowing.

Get your free resources

In addition to devouring this book, these resources will help you on your way to creating and sustaining a world-class coaching culture, so you boost employee engagement and drive results.

Get your FREE Coaching System Scorecard

Take the test (less than 10 minutes) to get your Scorecard – a fully customised report. It identifies the exact parts of a High-Performance Coaching system your contact centres are missing.

Go to www.bravatrak.com/scorecard

Subscribe to the 'Secrets to Contact Center Success' podcast

I interview the best and brightest minds in the contact centre industry about their latest and greatest tips. We discuss topics including employee engagement, customer experience, recruitment, retention, sales and much more.

Tune in on Apple Podcasts, Spotify or YouTube. Or go to www.bravatrak.com/podcast

Praise from clients
who have implemented the advice in this book

*Using the methods described in this book, we've helped many con-
tact centres and retail networks to boost employee engagement
and increase customer experience, productivity and sales performance. Here are quotes from some of the clients we've helped
over the past 25 years.*

"BravaTrak's High-Performance Coaching system creates
results which are immediate and tangible. Implementing it had
an amazing impact on sales, staff morale and retention, and the
whole culture of the Centre Network. We've had our best years
on record because of BravaTrak. I really think the missing link
has been found with this system."

*Trevor Pilkington, General Manager – Centre Network, New Zealand
Automobile Association*

"Within five months, 'call handling time' reduced from around
seven minutes to less than five minutes 30 seconds. This reduction led to a dramatic decrease in 'average wait time', improving
our clients' experience and enabling our clients to access more
support through the phone channel. We also made consider-
able savings in telecommunications costs. During this time staff
engagement also improved beyond the public sector benchmark."

*George Van Ooyen, Group General Manager Client Service Support at
New Zealand Ministry of Social Development*

"Two months after we implemented the BravaTrak system, there was more than a 200% increase in sales revenue. Within six months, there was more than a 400% increase. In 10 months, there was a 519% increase.

"During this time there was also a 34% reduction in unplanned leave, down from 572 to 376 lost days per month. This equated to an extra 10 staff being available. Employee engagement increased, and a positive change in morale and culture occurred."

Bryan Yianakis, former Director of Sales & Service, AAPT

"High-Performance Coaching helped us increase sales conversion by 25% within four months."

Susy Goldner, former Global Guest Contact Centre Manager, Virgin Australia Airlines

"We've found BravaTrak to be a tool to replicate the DNA of top leaders. We find out what our best leaders are doing, and then coach the others to help them improve. Since using BravaTrak, in addition to better business results, we now have a stronger, more engaged team that is following a plan. We have happier people, with greater resilience and commitment."

Todd Hunter, Chief Executive Officer, Turners Automotive Group

"Within 21 weeks of applying the BravaTrak system in two of our call centre campaigns, sales revenue increased by 278% in one of them, and by 281% in the other. When we applied it to another of our campaigns, sales conversion increased by 43% within a month."

Josh Ballantyne, former Sales Manager at a multinational insurance company

"Using BravaTrak's High-Performance Coaching system in our contact centres, 'call handle time' dropped by 65 seconds, 'quality of calls' went up – calibrated by an external Quality Auditor – and 'customer availability' increased from 50% to 95%. I estimate BravaTrak helped us create an annual saving of $300,000. But the important thing is we achieved better service levels with fewer staff. So not only did we reduce costs but we also improved time to answer calls from a customer perspective."

Dwina Dickinson, former Head of Retail Operations, Contact Energy

"Across the business, we saw an improvement in warranty sales of over 20% from using BravaTrak."

Craig Robertson, former General Manager Operations,
Noel Leeming Group

"The BravaTrak framework delivered a measurable and systematic approach to coaching, focusing on behaviours as the drivers of key business outcomes. It proved to be a key tool to help improve Telecom's Contact Centre culture and performance."

Trish Keith, former General Manager Customer Experience,
Telecom New Zealand (now Spark NZ)

"As a result of the productivity gains we got from using the BravaTrak system in our outbound collections centre, we reduced the number of staff from 48 to 33 (a 31% reduction), without reducing throughput. That's as good as money in the bank."

Jim Wrigley, former Australasian Collections Manager, ADT Security

"BravaTrak played a critical role in helping State Insurance achieve new growth in customer and policy numbers."

Mel Turdeich, former Contact Centre Sales Manager, State Insurance

"Before we used the BravaTrak system, the overall satisfaction rating of our agents was 78.5%, as measured by an ASAT (Agent Satisfaction) survey. Five months after implementation, overall satisfaction had already moved to 86.6%. After 12 months, agent satisfaction had increased further to 91%. Morale is now high and the overall atmosphere feels much more relaxed."

Benito Sy, former Director of Account Operations, Sitel

"Within four months, fundraising revenue from all channels in the program had doubled. Over the following 12 months, revenue increases across the five channels in the program ranged between 342% and 1,545%.

"Using the BravaTrak system also increased our employee engagement to a world-class level. Within four months, employee engagement had increased by 18%. Over the following 12 months, employee engagement improved by 37% and achieved the world best practice benchmark."

Devinia Liddelow, former People Capability & Change Manager, World Vision Australia

"The productivity improvements BravaTrak helped us achieve enabled us to reduce our headcount by eight full-time staff. At the same time, employee engagement for our division rose from amongst the lowest in the business to rivalling that of the senior leadership team – traditionally the most highly engaged group in the company."

Bashir Khan, National Manager of Business Membership & Contact Centres, New Zealand Automobile Association

"Working with BravaTrak enabled us to sign up more new plasma donors than we hoped for. There was a 40% increase in six months. As a result, we hit our Plasma Donor Panel stretch target more than a year early. A phenomenal achievement I never thought was possible."

Doug Gallagher, Director Donor Services, NZ Blood Service

2ND EDITION

GAME ON

How to create a
world-class coaching culture
so you boost engagement
and drive results

BLAIR STEVENSON
and the team at BravaTrak

Disclaimer
The material in this publication is of the nature of general comment only, and does not represent professional advice. It is not intended to provide specific guidance for particular circumstances and it should not be relied on as the basis for any decision to take action or not take action on any matter which it covers. Readers should obtain professional advice where appropriate, before making any such decision. To the maximum extent permitted by law, the author and publisher disclaim all responsibility and liability to any person, arising directly or indirectly from any person taking or not taking action based on the information in this publication.

CONTENTS

CONTENTS

I DIDN'T SIGN UP FOR THIS

Sales revenue well behind target

I didn't sign up for this, thought Sally Swift, her stomach in knots. She was on her fifth coffee of the day, and it wasn't even lunchtime. Her 26th-floor office afforded a view over the city and harbour beyond. As she looked out the window, Sally thought about the situation she was in. Sales revenue was well behind target. She was sure there was a way to increase sales performance and beat her targets, but she couldn't put her finger on what more she could do.

Sally had joined Velocity Inc. three months earlier as their General Manager of Contact Centres. The previous General Manager had left at short notice. Sales revenue had been dramatically reduced because of the Covid-19 pandemic and had not recovered. He eventually jumped ship before he was pushed.

Velocity had lured Sally away from a lesser role in a smaller company. They liked her because she had a reputation as a driven manager who achieved great results.

Although this new role was a step up for Sally, she'd felt confident she would succeed; but now, she wasn't sure.

She had thrown everything she knew into improving sales. The sales reporting hadn't been to her satisfaction, so she'd quickly had it fixed. And she made sure all her teams received sales training. The Human Resources team trained all her managers in a new coaching technique. She'd also put pressure on the heads of her inbound and outbound contact centres to lift performance.

These efforts helped Sally achieve a small lift in performance, but she was still far from reaching her targets. This failure wasn't just a problem for Velocity; it was starting to reflect poorly on her. Velocity's Chief Operating Officer, Doyle, had the board breathing down his neck, and so – as Sally's manager – he was beginning to make her life difficult.

Sales performance wasn't her only challenge. The key productivity measure in her inbound centres was 'grade of service'. Performance was well below the target of 80% of calls answered within 20 seconds. Moreover, customer experience was not where she needed it to be. And the latest employee engagement results had delivered further bad news: her division had the lowest engagement scores across the entire business.

So, things were not going well.

Paying the price

Sally was starting to pay the price of the pressure she was under. She hadn't been sleeping well lately, and felt guilty about how little time her husband, Michael, and their two children got from her.

As she looked out her office window, Sally noticed the lunch-time runners in the park below. They made her aware she hadn't had time for exercise in weeks.

At that moment, her phone buzzed. She checked the new message: "Looking forward to seeing you in 15! Alex."

It was Friday, and Sally was meeting an old friend for lunch. Alex was the Chief Executive at another company. They'd met at university and started their first jobs together. It had been months since they'd talked.

"See you soon," Sally messaged back, and checked her appearance in a small mirror before leaving. Her face looked more lined than usual. *Darn, I look tired*, she thought as she touched up her make-up.

On her way to lunch, Sally noticed dark clouds appearing overhead. She remembered the weather forecast was for heavy rain. Too late to bring an umbrella. Sally hurried on before the rain arrived. Almost at her destination, she heard someone call to her. It was Alex, dressed in a light blue suit. With her short, stylish haircut and designer glasses, she looked every bit the successful businesswoman she was.

"Hi Alex, it's wonderful to see you. It's been a while," said Sally.

"It certainly has," Alex said. They hugged and walked the short distance to Prego, which they considered the best deli in the city.

The delicious aromas of food and coffee greeted them as they entered. Sally adored the ambience of the place with its dark floor, solid wooden tables and modern rattan chairs. Both Alex and Sally were lovers of Prego's Cuban hot sandwich. The Cuban was cooked like a burger on a grill. Filled with pork and pickles and cheese, it packed a taste sensation. Sally ordered one for each of them, along with coffee for Alex. She didn't need any more caffeine today.

"Lunch is on me," Sally said. Alex knew better than to insist otherwise. She thanked Sally and took the cube of wood with their order number over to an empty table. It had a view of the street with its bumper-to-bumper traffic and busy pedestrians. The sunlight was fading.

When Sally joined her, Alex said, "You don't seem your normal self. You're lacking your usual spark." Sally sighed as she draped her red jacket over the chair. "Work's been a nightmare recently. But let's talk about that later. How've you been?"

Alex recounted her latest news, including how well things were going at work. As they talked, a steady stream of customers entered the deli and sat down. Their conversations gradually filled the place. Once their food arrived, the pair was silent for a moment while they savoured their first bite.

Alex was the first to talk again. "You mentioned earlier it's been a nightmare for you recently. What's been going on?"

"You'll remember I started with a new company three months' ago."

"You now run the contact centres for Velocity, as I recall … " Alex took another bite of her Cuban. She noticed it had begun to rain outside.

"That's right. By the way, this is all in the strictest of confidence."

Alex nodded. *Of course.*

Sally told Alex that her biggest challenge was figuring out how to grow sales revenue. She explained how it had been in decline for many months before she came in due to the pandemic, but she had managed to turn things around and get a small improvement. But, to her dismay, nothing she had done had lifted sales enough. Customer experience and productivity were also suffering. On top of all that, her division was now infamous for having the company's worst employee engagement.

Alex leaned forward and placed a consoling hand over Sally's. "You've only been there three months. I'd say you've made a good start."

"Maybe, but my channel handles 40% of our total revenue, so I'm feeling pressure from above. I report to the Chief Operating Officer, Doyle. He's good with numbers, but not so good with people. My head will be on the chopping block in the next few months if I don't lift sales significantly."

The sudden sound of heavy rain on the iron roof interrupted their discussion. They paused for a moment as they waited for the noise to abate. Once it did, Alex took up the conversation.

A lifeline

"You should talk to James Brava," she said. "He ran our national contact centres brilliantly for a couple of years. I haven't met another senior manager who's achieved improvements in sales, productivity and customer experience as great as he did for us. Performance consistently exceeded targets under his leadership. Also, employee engagement across his contact centres ended up rivalling our senior leadership team. I haven't seen that happen anywhere else."

To Sally, James sounded too good to be true. As it happened, Alex had also been sceptical when James applied for the role.

"He used to be a management consultant. He specialised in helping contact centres maximise their performance by establishing a world-class coaching culture," Alex explained. "The case studies he provided showed astonishing increases in performance. Frankly, I didn't believe them at first. It wasn't until I talked with some of his past clients that I realised he was the real deal."

"A world-class coaching culture?"

"James likes to take an evidence-based approach to his work. He says the data clearly shows that frontline teams led by the best coaches generate much greater customer satisfaction, productivity and sales revenue. The High-Performance Coaching System he developed blends behavioural science and strategy execution techniques to improve performance."

Sally picked at a rogue pickle that had fallen onto her plate. "If he's so good, why did he leave what was presumably a well-paid consulting gig to work for you?"

Alex said that James had retired from management consulting, but after a few months he'd become rather bored and wanted something to do. Unfortunately for Alex, he'd retired again about six months ago and was now in demand as a conference speaker.

Alex wiped her hands on her napkin and removed a business card and pen from her bag. "Let me give you his number. Hopefully he's around, but even if he's not, you can easily video conference with him. James owes me a big favour. Tell him you're calling it in."

"Thanks, Alex. I really appreciate your help." Sally paused for a moment, looking out the window. Then she pulled her notebook out of her bag and made a quick note, and put the notebook back in her bag.

"It looks like the rain has passed. Let's make a move while we still can," said Sally.

"Good idea."

As they left Prego, the sun started to shine. They could smell the fresh rain on the wet tarmac. "Thanks for a wonderful lunch," said Alex. "It was great to see you again. Love to Michael."

"You're welcome. It was fabulous to see you too. I'll let you know how I get on."

Back in her office, Sally put the business card aside. She'd arranged meetings to debrief her managers on their poor employee engagement results. But when she returned late in the day, she dialled the number Alex had provided.

A male voice answered. It was James. Sally introduced herself and explained that Alex had recommended she call him. With a little encouragement from James, she told him about the challenges she was facing, then went on to describe how overwhelmed she was feeling and the personal impact the situation was having on her.

Hearing the desperation in her voice, James suggested they meet as soon as possible, asking if she played golf. They could meet tomorrow morning for a game. Sally paused, thinking she'd have to miss her son and daughter's soccer game in the morning. However, she could make it up to them in the afternoon.

"I do. I'm a member at Northbridge," she said.

"Terrific. I haven't played there for a long time. Let's meet outside the clubhouse at nine. Does that suit you?"

"Sounds like an excellent plan. I look forward to talking with you then."

Sally's notes

Call James Brava to find out how to create a world-class coaching culture with his High-Performance Coaching system.

CHAPTER 2

AN INTRODUCTION TO HIGH-PERFORMANCE COACHING

"I need some quick wins"

Shortly before nine the following day, Sally waited outside the Northbridge clubhouse. It was a crisp, bright day, and the dew on the fairway glistened in the morning sun. *Hopefully, the ground isn't too wet from yesterday's rain*, she thought. As she looked around, she noticed a slim older man walking her way. He wore a white cap, and a black golf bag hung from his shoulder.

"You must be Sally," he said, extending a hand.

"And you must be James. Thanks for coming. I'm very grateful for you taking the time to see me."

"My pleasure," he said. "I see you've got your clubs. Shall we get going?"

Sally had already signed them on for the round, so they headed straight to the first tee. Ralph's Pride was the name of the first hole and was a par 4. Looking down the fairway, they could see a group of golfers in the distance. They were slowly disappearing behind some trees as they made their way to the green.

James teed off first.

As Sally practised her swing, James noticed red appeared to be her favourite colour. She wore a red polo shirt and red lipstick, and her golf shoes had striking red highlights. Even her golf tees and the fluffy covers on her clubs were red.

Sally teed off, and they followed their balls down the fairway.

"I'm sure Alex has told you a bit about my background," James said as they walked. "Tell me about yourself."

"After university I went into sales. I found I enjoyed working in contact centres; initially as a customer service rep and then as a team leader. I was fortunate enough to be able to take time off when my children came along. When I returned to work, I took a contact centre manager role with Supreme for five years. I had a great time there, but the offer from Velocity was too tempting to turn down."

They paused their conversation to complete their second strokes. Then Sally went on to tell him her new role had been a much more significant step up than she'd expected. With a long sigh, she said it felt like she'd been there for three years rather than three months.

By now they had rounded the corner and were chipping their balls onto the green. The blue flag marking the hole fluttered in the gentle breeze. Sally finished the hole one stroke over par, while James finished two over, by which time Sally had explained the situation she faced at Velocity and what she'd done during her first 90 days.

"That gives me excellent insight," James said. "So, what help would you like from me?"

"I need our performance to improve much more quickly than it has been. The pressure is starting to get to me, and I'm spending no time with my family. I need some quick wins, and Alex tells me you believe that building a coaching culture is the answer."

"Definitely." He paused for a moment and then continued, "How about I show you how to create a world-class coaching culture by putting a High-Performance Coaching system in place? That will go a long way to helping you solve the problems you're facing. I can also act as a sounding board for you along the way. Would that help?"

"Sounds perfect!" said Sally, starting to feel like maybe she was on to something.

They followed a snaking path to the second tee, a short distance away. James went first from the back tee, and once Sally had teed off, the pair walked on.

James asked, "What data do you have on the coaching your team leaders are doing?"

"How do you mean?"

"How are you tracking the coaching your team leaders are providing their agents and how well they're doing it?"

"We're not. Why do you ask?"

"Your team leaders hold the key to your success," James explained. "Their coaching activity directly affects their teams' performance. Put bluntly, how well you do depends on your most junior and least-experienced managers.

If I were you, I'd want to know what coaching they were doing and how well they were doing it."

Sally stood mute. *How did I miss that?* she thought.

Systems

James reached into his pocket and removed a sheet of folded paper. Once unfolded, he showed it to Sally and pointed to the diagram on the page. "Let's put the measurement of coaching activity aside for the moment. We can come back to it once we have the coaching fundamentals in place.

"There are five things you need to understand to embed a High-Performance Coaching system:

- what game you're playing

- how to win

- how to coach

- when to coach

- the need to referee the game."

Sally looked at the diagram. "This isn't what I was expecting at all," she said. "I thought High-Performance Coaching simply referred to the coaching techniques we should be using. What you have here is so much more than that."

James explained that most organisations took an ad-hoc approach to improving performance. They provided training to their frontline staff. Or they taught their managers a coaching technique. Or they ran an employee feedback survey. Each element was put in place separately from the others. But the key to consistently exceeding targets was to put a *system* in place.

High-Performance Coaching system

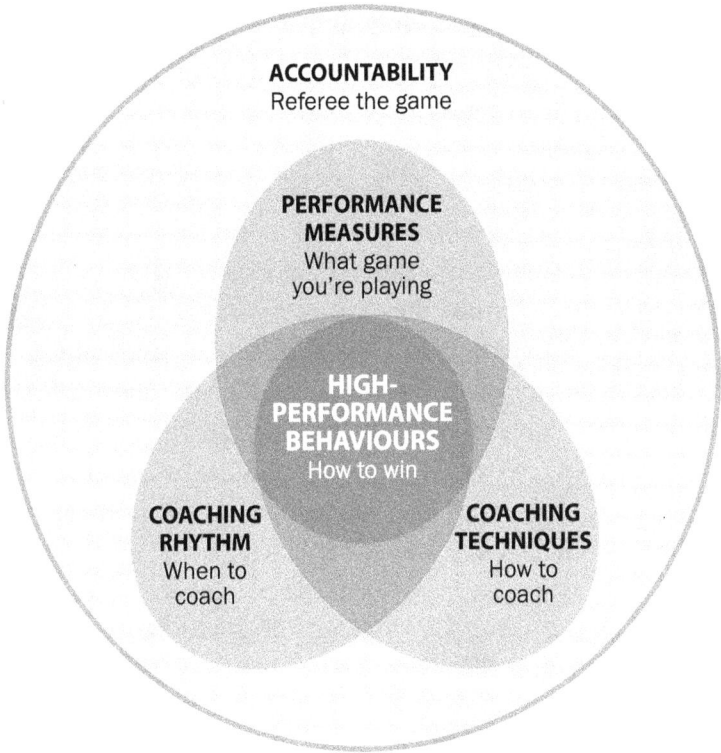

ACCOUNTABILITY
Referee the game

PERFORMANCE
MEASURES
What game
you're playing

HIGH-
PERFORMANCE
BEHAVIOURS
How to win

COACHING
RHYTHM
When to
coach

COACHING
TECHNIQUES
How to
coach

"Imagine you've boarded a flight," he said. "As you settle into your seat, the captain comes on the intercom to inform you the crew wouldn't be following the usual flight procedures today. They feel those systems are too constraining and don't take into account their individual nature. What's the likelihood you'd want to get off the plane?"

"One hundred percent," said Sally.

He went on to ask a similar question about Sally needing to have surgery. He asked her to imagine her reaction to the surgeon mentioning he didn't follow any system when operating. Instead, he preferred to freestyle it on the day. She laughed, saying she'd look for another surgeon.

"And so what's the chance," he inquired further, "the coaches of high-performing sports teams don't have systems to follow?"

She thought for a moment. "None at all," she replied. "Okay … you have my attention. You're saying we need a High-Performance Coaching system for our team leaders to follow to maximise their teams' performance."

"You're exactly right," James said and handed her the sheet of paper. Sally studied it while he searched for his ball in the long grass at the edge of the fairway. Once found, James chipped it out with an iron. The ball landed just short of the green. Sally followed suit, except her ball landed within centimetres of the hole.

After sinking an easy putt, Sally pointed to the High-Performance Coaching diagram. "This says our performance measures define the game we're playing. Improving customer experience and productivity is necessary, but since my priority is to increase sales revenue, that's the game we're playing."

Determining the game you're playing

"You're both right and wrong," replied James. "You're right in that your performance measures determine the game you're playing. But you're wrong to think the game you're playing is solely about increasing sales revenue. That will only cause you a world of hurt."

Sally turned towards him, looking confused.

"There are two types of performance measures," James explained. "The results that define success for your business are one type. You'll normally describe your strategic goals at this level. The objectives that enable those business results are the other. Sales revenue is a business result. Unfortunately, it's not something you can manage directly."

Sally shook her head. "That doesn't make any sense to me. Nor will you convince my boss of that. It's the only thing he cares about."

James smiled. "Bear with me for a moment," he said. "Imagine sales revenue starts increasing. Thinking more widely, what might cause that to happen?"

"Well, the senior leadership team and the board have been working on a new strategy. That might be starting to work for us. We might have improved our marketing, or done more advertising." Sally paused and thought for a moment before continuing. "It's possible the economy has picked up, or interest rates have dropped. Alternatively, one of our competitors may have taken a hit to their reputation. Their customers could be flocking to us."

"All those things are possible," said James. "To what extent do your agents have any influence over these factors?"

Sally rubbed her temples for a moment, then looked up and gave him a reluctant smile. "All right, I get it. We can't directly manage our frontline teams on their sales revenue."

"No, you can't. I know everyone in your business closely tracks your business results. However, your front-line teams have much more influence over the objectives which contribute to increasing sales revenue."

"I'm not sure how … "

"Let's finish this hole, so we don't hold up the other players coming through … " James pointed to a wooden bench overlooking the green. "Then we can take a seat and continue our conversation."

Sally felt herself starting to relax. The quiet and green of the golf course helped, but it was mostly the growing feeling that salvation might be at hand.

Sally's notes

What is High-Performance Coaching?

High-Performance Coaching is a <u>system</u> for maximising the performance of our frontline teams:

- what game we're playing
- how we win
- how we coach
- when we coach
- I need to referee the game.

CHAPTER 3

UNDERSTANDING WHAT TO FOCUS ON

Results and objectives

The bench seat sat above a natural amphitheatre, with the green below at its centre. The ground climbed away from the green to their right. To their left were two sand traps, with the fairway beyond.

Once they were seated, Sally resumed the conversation. "You've made the point that we can influence objectives, but we can't directly manage results. What's an example of an objective?"

"Conversion rate is one example. Your agents influence that through what they say during their sales conversations. Save rate is another example. It's influenced in the same way by your agents. A further example is the number of sales calls completed. Your agents influence that through their effort. The same goes for their availability and average handling time."

Sally appeared disconcerted. "Maybe I haven't thought this stuff through enough. We already report on a range of performance measures that include a mix of what you call results and objectives. But since the board and my boss are so focused on sales revenue, I've put the emphasis there. So … the performance measures describe the game we're playing," she concluded.

"That's right. The results and objectives together dictate the game you're playing."

As they talked, a group of four players made their way onto the green below. The pair paused to watch them putt, and then Sally picked up the conversation again.

"How does this work for performance measures other than sales?"

"What do you have in mind?"

"We use net promoter score as a measure of customer experience. One of my goals is to substantially increase NPS over the next 12 months. It's just dawned on me that NPS is a business result influenced by a huge number of factors. So, it's not something we can directly manage."

"You're right. From the data you have, what are the areas customers are telling you need improvement?"

"The biggest issue is we don't always call our customers back with the information they need by the date we promised. So, the objective might be the percentage of follow-ups completed by the promised date. We could track that through our CRM system. Customer satisfaction as a contributor to customer experience could be an objective we address later."

James agreed they were good examples of objectives. Her agents could influence them through their actions.

Sally leaned over to her golf bag and removed her small red notebook from a side pocket. She made a note in it before continuing. "The other challenge I have is lifting the grade of service in my inbound centres. Several things outside the control of our agents affect that result. However, agents can influence it through their average call handling time. So that could be one objective."

Change takes effort

"Good, you've got the concept," he said. "Let's now take it further. Change always takes effort, so it's difficult to get people to change too much at once. You need to decide on a priority result on which to get your people focused."

"As I've mentioned, I'm facing a few challenges."

"I understand that, but when you try to change everything, nothing changes. You'll need to focus on one priority result at a time if you want to be successful. The easy way to identify your priority is to answer a straightforward question: if performance in everything else were to remain the same, what's the one result area where change would have the greatest impact?"

"Sales revenue," Sally replied without hesitation. "Right now I have to grow that." She paused for a moment to reflect. "So I guess we need to identify the objectives that have the biggest impact on revenue. What do you think they are?"

James drummed his fingers on the wooden bench. While he was thinking, Sally took in the view. She noticed a passenger jet tracking across the sky. *Probably off to somewhere tropical*, she thought. Someplace she and Michael needed to go to get some relaxation and time together.

James's voice brought her back to their discussion. "I recommend you limit yourself to only one or two enabling objectives, so you need to make sure you select the right ones. Any more and your teams will lose focus. The objectives need to lead to the achievement of your priority result. And your frontline staff must have significant influence over them."

"Could we have different objectives for inbound and outbound?"

"Yes, you should deal with your inbound and outbound teams separately. Your inbound service centres might make sales themselves. Alternatively, they might generate leads for someone else to follow up at a later date."

Sally nodded. "Having our customer service agents generate leads would be best. We've been moving our better salespeople to outbound. So, the outbound relationship teams can do the follow-up. They'll have more time to make sure we're meeting customer needs. It also fits nicely with our strategy of selling more products to existing customers. Those sales cost us a lot less to make. Customers are also less likely to move to a competitor if they have several products with us."

"So the first enabling objective for your inbound service teams is 'lead generation'," James said. "Now let's think about your outbound teams. The obvious enabling objective for your sales agents would be 'sales conversion rate'. What do you think?"

Sally agreed.

James laid out some action points for Sally for the coming week. He suggested she work with her inbound teams to identify one or two products for which they would focus on generating more leads. With her outbound teams, James suggested she identify one or two products for which they would initially focus on improving sales conversion. He also recommended checking if any productivity issues were holding back performance, such as agent availability.

"I'll get started Monday morning!" Sally said. She again looked at the sheet of paper James had given her earlier. "In the meantime, I'd also appreciate some guidance on how to win, which I see links to what you've called high-performance behaviours."

"I can help you there … It looks like there's a gap between that last group of golfers and the next. How about we jump back into our game? We can walk and talk."

The third hole was called Silver Lake. The black plaque with gold lettering said it was a par 3. There was a lake in front of them, curving to the left of the green. James said he'd undercooked his shot last time on this hole, and ended up in the water. But he wasn't going to repeat that today. With a powerful swing, his ball soared … over the green, over the sand trap and into the trees beyond. With a sigh, he returned the club to his bag.

Sally hit her ball well, and it stopped within a couple of metres of the hole.

"Good shot," said James. "You have great form, particularly turning your left shoulder behind the ball on your backswing."

The ROAM model

He asked Sally for the paper with the High-Performance Coaching system diagram.

"This is called the ROAM model," he said as he drew on the back of the sheet.

"Because … you use it while hiking?" Sally joked.

"No," said James, smiling. "It stands for 'results, objectives, activities and method'."

The ROAM model

Performance measures
} **R**esults

Objectives

High-Performance behaviours
} **A**ctivities

Method

"Let me show you how performance measures and high-performance behaviours are tied together. A wide range of factors affect your business results, many of which are outside the control of your teams. However, your teams influence performance in the objectives that enable the achievement of those results. The number of sales leads generated is one example you mentioned. But agents can only generate leads when they do certain activities. Your team leaders can manage how they do these activities."

"'Attempting to generate leads' is the obvious activity for the inbound teams," Sally said.

"I agree. As for your outbound sales teams, what activities contribute to sales conversion?"

"That's less obvious to me."

"Let me give you one or two suggestions, and you can discuss them with your team."

Sally turned to a new page in her notebook.

"What key skills were emphasised in the recent sales training workshops?" James asked.

"I was reminded of the importance of following a proven sales process to identify customer needs. I guess that's the activity that contributes to sales conversion."

James suggested the activity could be made more specific by describing how sales agents should identify customer needs.

She said, "They have to ask questions to uncover the problems our customers are experiencing that we can solve. They also need to ask questions to identify the impact of the customer's problem. The more serious the problem, the more likely a customer is to take action."

James nodded. "In that case, you could frame the activity as 'asking questions to identify customer needs'." Looking around, he continued, "We're falling behind with all this talking. How about we continue over a coffee once we've finished our game?"

Sally's notes

Results and objectives: the game we're playing

We need to get the ROAM model in place: Results and Objectives (the game we're playing); Activities and Method (how to win).

Results = Performance measures which our frontline teams can't control

Objectives = Performance measures our frontline team members can influence

Focus on one priority result at a time and the one or two enabling objectives which significantly impact it.

Example #1

Priority result = Net promoter score (NPS)

Enabling objective = Percentage of follow-ups completed by the promised date

Example #2

Priority result = Grade of service (GOS)

Enabling objective = Average call handling time

For our inbound contact centres

Priority result = Sales revenue

Enabling objective = Lead generation

For our outbound contact centres

Priority result = Sales revenue

Enabling objective = Sales conversion rate

CHAPTER 4

HOW TO KEEP SCORE

After they'd played the final hole, Sally and James walked up the slope to the clubhouse. It was just before 1:30 pm. Neither was hungry as they'd both eaten sandwiches as they'd played.

No-one was sitting outside under the shade sail. With plenty of choices, they picked a table overlooking the 18th green. James put his scorecard down and went inside to order, while Sally took a seat at the end of the table. The spot gave her sweeping views of the clubhouse on one side and the expanse of the course on the other. While she was waiting for James to return, she added up their scores.

"How'd we do?" James asked when he came back.

Sally had a broad smile. "You shot 113 and an 89 for me."

James took off his golf cap and ran his fingers through his short hair. "You had the better game today – that's for sure."

Sally noticed a young woman approaching with their coffees.

"Oh, thanks. Put them right here." Sally moved the scorecards to make room. After the waitress had left, she stirred the two sugar cubes from her saucer into her long black.

Keeping score

James leaned forward as he took a sip of coffee. "Talking about our scores is a good introduction to the last thing I wanted to discuss with you today."

Sally tilted her head slightly to her left: "What's that?"

"Keeping score. As a matter of interest, what team sports do you follow?"

"Soccer. It's a family favourite since my son and daughter play," said Sally.

"Imagine you're in the stands at a big game. Is there any time in the game when you don't know the score?"

"No. The scoreboard is always updated when a goal's scored."

"What would happen if no-one knew the score?" James asked. The seat he'd chosen left him out in the heat of the sun. He moved places, so he was sitting in the cool shadow of the shade sail.

Sally waited until he settled, then replied, "If no-one knew the score, the game would have no purpose, and nobody would be able to make any decisions." She paused for a moment. "That's why I've worked so hard on improving our sales reporting. But you seem to be suggesting we give our frontline teams immediate visibility of their performance."

"More or less," he said. "There are several good reasons for doing so."

At that moment loud talking from the 18th green distracted them. Sally and James could see a group of men completing their round. They were congratulating each other on their scores and how well they'd played.

James raised his arm in their direction and continued. "As you can hear, keeping score prompts people to celebrate each other's achievements. That motivates them to do even better. It also means players can see when they're off track. As a result, they're more likely to self-correct and ask for help when they've got a problem."

"You're saying people need to see the progress they're making. And when they do, they're more motivated to improve."

He smiled and told her she'd summarised the point nicely.

Visibility of performance

"Once we've finalised our performance measures, we can create scoreboards for our frontline teams in our dashboard software. But I don't have the budget for large wall-mounted monitors to display real-time updates to each team. Until I do, how could we give our frontline teams that visibility?"

"Simple. You could use hand-drawn scoreboards to track team performance in the priority result and the one or two enabling objectives." James asked for Sally's red notebook so he could draw an example. "Your priority result is sales revenue. Let's say your enabling objective is lead generation. There are 20 working days in the month, and each team's target is 200 leads for the month. Here's how a team scoreboard might look for lead generation."

Team scoreboard example

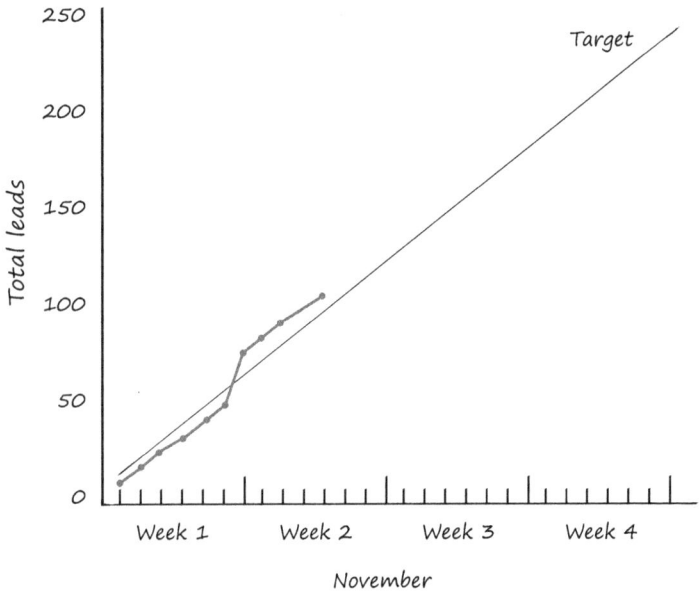

"If you use this approach, all teams could see how they're performing against their target each day. The best place to put the scoreboard is on a wall where everyone can see it. The bigger, the better."

"What about providing visibility of individual performance, as we get with these?" asked Sally as she gestured to the golf scorecards they'd used.

"Team leaders need to supply that information every day to each of their team members. The easiest way is to compile a table showing each team member's performance in the enabling objectives for the previous day. That can be emailed to their team each morning."

"Right," she said. "I'll meet with my team on Monday to agree to the objectives and activities we'll focus on. We'll also figure out what scoreboards we'll put in place."

"While you're doing that, give some thought to your targets. For your priority result, identify your goal and the date you want to achieve it by. For your enabling objectives, identify the performance level you think is achievable. The performance of your top-performing frontline staff will help you figure out what's possible."

"Can do. We should be ready by mid-week to talk to you about how our method fits into your ROAM model. Can we meet on Wednesday?"

"Sure. When and where?"

Sally finished her coffee. "I'll call you Tuesday to let you know." She stood to shake hands. "Thanks for the game, and for helping me out today."

She left him to enjoy the last of his coffee, while she headed home to spend time with her family.

Sally's notes

Scoreboards: how to track the game we're playing

Scoreboards are essential because keeping score:

- helps people know if they're winning or losing
- motivates them to do better
- prompts people to celebrate each other's achievements
- encourages them to put in more effort when they're off track.

Team scoreboards

These show team performance on the priority result and enabling objectives.

Make them large. Scoreboards should be on the wall where all team members can see them.

Individual scoreboards

These show the performance of all team members in each enabling objective.

Have team leaders share updates by email.

CHAPTER 5

OFF TO A GREAT START

But still working late

Sally called James on Tuesday evening. She was still at her desk, and she was worn out. James had just finished an hour-long video chat with a relative in Spain and was preparing himself a drink. One finger of whiskey topped with soda.

"I could do with one of those," Sally said. Through the phone she could hear the tinkle of ice in a glass.

"Tell me how things are going," he said, as he settled into his favourite chair – an old high-back armchair clad in well-worn leather.

"Yesterday's meeting with Doyle didn't go nearly as well as I thought it would. On the one hand, he's reassured I have a plan. On the other, he's sceptical the plan will deliver the fast improvement in sales revenue he wants. He's given me a week to come up with more specifics about how I'm going to increase sales."

"You've bought yourself some time then."

"But I need to keep moving. I spent today with my heads of inbound and outbound, Jo-Anne and Mark, to decide our focus. We confirmed what you and I discussed on Saturday. Our priority result is sales revenue. We want to be achieving $3.5 million in new sales revenue every month by the 30th of April. For inbound, our first enabling objective is leads generated for Funeral Cover. It's a new product with compelling benefits. We're currently averaging 41 leads per agent per month. We want that up to 100 leads each month within four months. The activity will clearly be 'attempting to generate Funeral Cover leads'."

Sally stifled a yawn. After twelve hours at work, she was running on empty.

"Perfect. Do you have any other enabling objective?" James asked, and then took a sip of whiskey.

Sally put her mobile on the desk and switched to speaker before replying. "We talked about the low agent availability across Jo-Anne's inbound teams. They're supposed to be available to talk with customers at least 80% of their rostered time. We're currently averaging around 75%. We want that up to 83% within the next three months. If we can do that, our agents will be available for 10% more time, which should give us more opportunity to generate leads. We think the key activity is 'logging in before the rostered time'."

"That's terrific progress, Sally. What about your outbound teams?"

"Give me a moment. I'll be right back," said Sally. The office cleaners had arrived with their vacuum cleaners.

Closing the door and turning back to the desk, she noticed night had fallen. The twinkling lights of the city spread before her. *I should be at home with Michael and the kids*, Sally thought.

"It's more straightforward with outbound," she continued. "We've decided to focus on improving sales conversion of two products. One of them is our Fairweather product, for which we mostly receive sales leads from internet enquiries. The other is Funeral Cover. We'll be receiving more sales leads for that from inbound. We'd like to be hitting a 45% conversion rate each month by the 28th of February. That seems achievable based on what our best sales agents are doing."

"Good. What activities will influence sales conversion?"

"Weeeeeeellllllll," said Sally, drawing the word out. "We had a long discussion about that. We're not fully clear on them yet, and I'm hoping you'll be able to help us. For the moment we'll focus on asking questions to identify customer needs as we discussed."

"You've made an excellent start," James said, sounding pleased. "What have you decided to do about using scoreboards?"

A photo of Sally's family sat in a silver frame on her desk. She looked at it as she talked. The sight of her three favourite people gave her energy.

"Jo-Anne and Mark are meeting with their centre managers and team leaders tomorrow afternoon. They'll discuss the priority result and their enabling objectives. They'll also get agreement on the best way to display the scoreboards. We're aiming to have them in place by next Monday and have team leaders update them every day. We also thought about how we could provide more real-time visibility of team performance while we're waiting for the wall-mounted monitors."

"Very good."

"Mark mentioned that at his previous job, the leaders of the best-performing teams would email updates of team and individual performances throughout the day, not just at the start of the day as we talked about. So as of next Monday, we'll expect all team leaders to do the same. They'll easily be able to do it three times a day with our new sales reporting."

"That's ideal. You're off to a great start."

"Thanks. It's taken some effort to get here," Sally said wearily. "Before Jo-Anne and Mark meet with their teams tomorrow afternoon, we'd like to meet with you to understand your ROAM model in more detail. Naturally, I've covered off results, objectives and activities with them. We'd now like to understand the final step. What's the chance we could meet in the morning?"

"Let me check." There was a pause as James checked his calendar. "I could meet you any time after ten o'clock."

"In that case, let's meet at ten-fifteen at my office. You know where we are?"

"I believe you're across the road from Hyde Park."

"That's right. See you then."

Sally's notes

The ROAM model for our contact centres

We've got Result, Objective, and Activity sorted. We now need Method!

Across all our contact centres

Priority result = Sales revenue. Target is $3.5 million in new monthly sales revenue by 30th April.

For our inbound contact centres

Enabling objective = Lead generation for Funeral Cover. Target is 100 leads per month per FTE within four months.

Activity = Attempting to generate Funeral Cover leads.

Enabling objective = Agent availability. Target is 83% availability within three months.

Activity = Logging in before rostered time.

For our outbound contact centres

Enabling objectives = Sales conversion rate for Fairweather and Funeral Cover. Target is 45% monthly conversion rate within four months.

Activity = Asking questions to identify customer needs.

CHAPTER 6

OBSERVING BEHAVIOUR

The next step

James called Sally to suggest a change of plan shortly before they were due to meet. He told her it would be more helpful to hold their discussion in Hyde Park. There was an opportunity to show Sally and her team a live example of how to identify high-performance behaviour.

Hyde Park occupied an area equal to ten city blocks. It was a giant green space filled with open grassy areas and playing fields. Various sculptures and statues could be found among the trees and crisscrossing paths. Since it was located on the edge of the central business district, the park was a magnet for office workers and tourists alike.

Sally and her team felt the warmth of the spring sun as they walked. Through the traffic she spotted James sitting on a stone wall near where they'd agreed to meet. Casually dressed in chinos and a polo shirt, he stood out in a sea of suits.

The group walked down to the pedestrian crossing on the nearby corner. Once across the road, they walked past a group of young fundraisers standing outside the main entrance to the park. The fundraisers wore bright yellow T-shirts and yellow hats. They were giving away small flower pins to everyone who donated. Two of them were sharing a bottle of sunscreen, which they were applying to their arms and faces.

"Hi there James," Sally called out, and introduced Mark and Jo-Anne.

James took off his sunglasses and shook hands. He noticed Mark was short and chubby and filled out his dark blue business suit. In contrast, Jo-Anne was tall and thin. She wore a black and white dress.

James suggested they go into the park to take advantage of the shade provided by the towering trees. They found two benches facing each other across a narrow path. One was unoccupied, and a young professional couple was just leaving the other. Sally and Jo-Anne sat on one side, facing the fundraisers on the corner. The men sat on the other.

Describing behaviour

Mark and Jo-Anne started the conversation, saying they understood results, objectives and activities. They now wanted to know more about method.

"Before we get into it, there's something I want to show you," James said. "Your sales method needs to describe the *behaviours* you want from your agents. So, to start with, let's make sure we're all on the same page when it comes to describing behaviour."

Sally noticed several of the fundraisers walking in their direction. They all had long hair and wore colourful friendship bracelets, guys and girls alike.

"I define behaviour as an observable action – something you can hear a person say or see them do," James said. "Would you agree with that?"

They all nodded. James zipped open the black leather folder on his knees and wrote in large letters the words:

Behaviour = Observable action (what people do or say)

He showed it to Mark and then held it up for Sally and Jo-Anne to see.

"Then let's have a go at identifying behaviour. Mark, would you be willing to help me out?"

"Sure," Mark said. The trees around them stirred in the breeze, causing the light and shadow to shimmer. Mark squinted as the light played across his eyes.

"Take a look at the charity fundraisers over there. See the guy with glasses?" James pointed with his pen. "What are a couple of behaviours he's using?"

Mark leaned forward to look past James. "He's confidently approaching people walking past him. He's also friendly."

James dropped his pen into the valley of his folder. "Thanks, Mark. Sally, remind me of our definition of behaviour."

"It's an observable action. Something you can hear a person say or see them do."

"Good," said James. "Mark said the guy is 'confidently approaching people'. Is the word 'confident' a description of his behaviour, or is it something else?"

Behaviour or judgement?

A few seconds of silence followed.

"Ah … no," Mark eventually said, grinding his right heel in the gravel on the path. "It wasn't a physical action he did or something he said. I guess it's my personal opinion."

"You're right. You made two judgements. That he's *confidently* approaching people, and that he's *friendly* to them. They're your *personal opinions* based on the behaviours you observed. So what did he *do* or *say* that caused you to form those judgements?"

Mark watched the fundraiser again as he approached people walking past him. "It looks like he faces towards the person he's targeting. He makes eye contact with them when they're five to ten metres away, and smiles at them. Then he lifts his arm above his shoulder on the side they're passing just before he starts talking to them."

"That's what I'm noticing as well. You've got the idea." James paused. "You also said he was friendly."

"That was a judgement too," Mark said, crossing his legs. "I said that because the guy's smiling at the people he approaches."

"Nice work. It takes practice to be behaviourally specific. Most managers speak in judgements with their team without any thought. For example, they might ask their team to 'proactively offer solutions', 'provide friendly service', or 'understand the customer's needs'."

Sally rubbed her temples from weariness. "What's the problem with that?" she asked. With the bigger challenges she faced, this level of detail seemed rather academic.

"Speaking in judgements makes our communication unclear. It also harms our ability to motivate people."

Sally said she didn't understand.

"In that case, let's explore it further. Imagine you're a frontline agent. Your team leader says to you 'great work on being friendly with that customer'. What's the behaviour they're recognising?"

Sally paused, looking at a stylish young father pushing a baby stroller along the path. The baby laughed and waved at the group, and they waved back. Once they had passed, Sally replied. "It's unclear what being 'friendly' refers to. I see what you mean — describing one or two specific actions would help me understand exactly what I've done well."

"Yes. Let's also think of a situation where your immediate manager wants to correct your behaviour. Imagine they say 'you're not a team player'. Mark, what's your reaction going to be?"

Mark raised his eyebrows. "I'd be defensive because that's their personal opinion. I'd disagree because they've offered no evidence. And I'd become demotivated and put less effort into my work."

Sally spoke up. "So James, you're saying we need to specify the *behaviours* we want people to use?"

"Yes. You need to clearly describe the behaviours that make the biggest difference to performance. I call them the 'high-performance behaviours'."

"There are two potential benefits to this approach, as I see it," Mark said. "It would allow us to let our agents and team leaders know what works best. It's also likely to help us avoid unethical sales practices by our agents."

"Tell me more," James said.

Mark replied, "In my last company, we used a high commission rate to incentivise our sales teams. We accidentally ended up creating a lot of unethical behaviour. We had sales agents not fully disclosing information to our customers. Some were misrepresenting our products and trying to close the sale at all costs." He went on to explain that those actions had given the company a bad name. But he also accepted it was the leadership team's fault because they had demanded better results without making it clear how they were to be achieved.

"We can combat that by helping our agents understand the specific behaviours to use to achieve the results we expect," he said. "If we do that, our team leaders will also know what behaviours to coach."

"You're exactly right," James said. "But before you can do that, you need to get good at specifying behaviour."

Sally's notes

Method: how to win

Behaviour vs Judgements

The method describes the behaviours that comprise each activity.

Behaviour = an observable action (what a person does or says). e.g. turns to face a person, makes eye contact, smiles.

VS

Judgement = a personal opinion. e.g. that a person is confident, or is friendly.

Using judgements makes our communication unclear. It also harms our ability to motivate people to improve their performance.

We need to specify the high-performance behaviours we expect team members to use and managers to coach. Then they'll be clear on how to achieve the results we expect.

CHAPTER 7

IDENTIFYING HIGH-PERFORMANCE BEHAVIOUR

Behaviour or outcome?

"Jo-Anne, you're up next. Provided you're comfortable with that," said James. She said she was willing to help out.

"Let's stay with these fundraisers. What are some of the behaviours the girl with long red hair is using?"

Jo-Anne looked over to where the young people were standing. "Hmm. She just got a small donation."

James adjusted his sunglasses. "Is that a behaviour or an outcome?"

Jo-Anne cocked her head to one side, thinking. "It's an outcome."

James explained that when you were coaching someone, just focusing on the outcome you wanted them to achieve was a recipe for disappointment. It didn't help them understand how to achieve it. That's what a focus on behaviour helped solve. So what did Jo-Anne notice the red-haired girl did to get the donation?

"Let me go and find out," Jo-Anne said. She stood up and walked to the park entrance. From there Jo-Anne could watch what the girl did more closely. Sally sat back, took a couple of deep breaths and closed her eyes. Thinking about nothing in particular, she enjoyed the opportunity to relax for a moment.

James's voice brought her out of her quiet time. Opening her eyes, she found Jo-Anne had returned and was grinning widely.

"She makes eye contact with people when they're five to ten metres away," she reported. "And she smiles at them just like the other guy. What's interesting is the script she's using."

"What does she say?" Mark asked.

"She says, 'I'm collecting for the Cancer Council. Our corporate team normally asks businesses for a $300 donation, but I'm wondering if you'd be willing to donate just $2 today.' I'm amazed at how many donations she's getting."

James put his hand up to high-five Jo-Anne. "Good work on pinpointing exactly what she's saying," he said. "That's a great example of a high-performance behaviour. She's using $300 as a pricing anchor to make a $2 donation seem very small. You need to get to the same level of detail with the words and actions that make the biggest difference in your contact centres."

"Sounds like quite a bit of work," Jo-Anne said.

James shook his head. "It's not as much as you'd think. Before we dig into how to do it, let's develop your understanding of behaviour a little more."

Macro- and micro-behaviours

He turned to Sally. "You've said that asking more problem and impact questions could improve sales conversion in outbound."

"That's right."

"Is asking a problem question a behaviour, or is it something else?"

"It's a behaviour because it's something you can hear an agent ask," Mark said.

James agreed, but pointed out that 'asking a problem question' only provided a broad description of the behaviour. He asked Mark to put himself in the shoes of one of his agents. Imagine he was told to ask questions to identify the problems customers were experiencing, problems that could be solved by the purchase of contents insurance. James wondered what specific questions Mark would ask in that situation.

There was a long pause, and Mark's face reddened. He said, "I'm having trouble thinking of any." In embarrassment he picked at the flaking green paint on the bench, then stopped as he realised what he was doing.

"If you simply tell your agents to ask problem questions, they'll have the same trouble. The phrase 'asking problem questions' describes a 'macro-behaviour'. It's a broad description of what you want your agents to do. To help them succeed, you need to provide them with *specific examples* of what to say."

Two pigeons marched along the path towards Sally's feet. She stood abruptly and clapped her hands, causing the birds to fly off. Once she sat down again, she said, "I thought of an example just before those birds interrupted me. I could ask the customer, 'If you had a house fire without adequate insurance cover for your belongings, what difficulties would you face?'"

"Good example. That question is a 'micro-behaviour' because it's a description of precisely what you could say," James said.

"What's so important about the difference?" Jo-Anne asked.

"When you know the macro-behaviours in the sales process, you know broadly what your agents need to do. When you provide examples of the micro-behaviours that create success, they'll know what they need to do and say specifically to achieve high performance."

"On one hand, what you're saying makes sense," said Jo-Anne, playing with the large gold beads of her necklace. "But there's one thing that's been bothering me. Aren't we going too far? Isn't there a danger of micro-managing our people?"

"Micro-managing is the opposite of what we want to achieve. Ideally, you want to give your agents independence in their decision-making. But you need to provide them with a framework within which they can make their choices. For example, do you agree they need to understand what you expect them to achieve, and your expectations of how they go about that?"

"Yes, of course," she said.

"And do you think it's useful to provide your people with clarity about what actions will help them to succeed?"

Jo-Anne nodded her agreement.

"That's all I'm suggesting you do. Figure out what behaviours lead to success and then communicate your expectations regarding their use," James said.

"I understand. You're recommending we put a behavioural framework in place to guide our agents. I withdraw my objection," Jo-Anne replied with a smile.

Gathering information

Mark said, "Our sales process is a good starting point for identifying the macro-behaviours. But the micro-behaviours are more specific to our products. How do we work those out?"

"What have we done today to identify high-performance behaviours?" asked James.

Mark smiled to himself, noticing how James was coaching him to come up with the answers. "We've been observing these fundraisers. We could do the same and observe some of our high-performing agents to find out what problem and impact questions they ask."

James agreed, saying that Mark was sure to have some agents achieving a much higher sales conversion rate than others. He could arrange for someone to observe several of them. From there it would be easy to find the commonalities in what they did and said. Once he had all his agents using the same micro-behaviours, James guaranteed that sales conversions would increase.

Looking around the park, Sally could see a groundskeeper on an orange ride-on mower disappear behind the spray of a fountain. There was a group of mothers with young children. The children were busy chasing and falling over each other. *It's been a long time since I've had a picnic with Michael and the children,* she thought. Mark's voice brought her back to the conversation.

"I can organise that. We can also make sure we include our standards of ethical conduct," Mark said.

"That's a smart move. You'll also find it worthwhile questioning your high performers while you're doing the observations. While some will be unaware of exactly what's working for them, others will know."

"Good idea."

James gave them an example of how useful the approach could be. He said he remembered once asking an agent who regularly had 85% availability about how she did it. She'd told him her rule was to be back at her workstation from breaks one minute before she was due.

Sally rubbed the brass studs securing the wooden planks of the bench. "That *is* simple. Is it common to have just a few micro-behaviours making such a difference?"

"I've come across it a few times," James said. "But usually there's between three and ten."

"Okay. What other approaches could I take?" Mark asked.

"Find a team leader who already knows the micro-behaviours and ask them."

"You know, I was reviewing our reporting yesterday," Mark said. "There's one team with a consistently high conversion rate."

"In that case, talk with the team leader. You may be surprised at what they can tell you about what works," James said.

Mark nodded.

James removed a fresh sheet of paper from his folder and started writing on it. He said, "Let's summarise the approaches you can use to identify high-performance behaviours. You'll want to use as many of them as possible."

He talked as he wrote:

Ways to identify high-performance behaviours:

1. Review your existing training materials.

2. Observe and interview your high performers.

3. Interview managers of high-performing teams.

4. Access information on best practice if it's available.

James continued: "Jo-Anne, we're going to use this last approach to help you figure out the lead generation method for your team. Since I have more than 20 years' cross-selling experience, I'm going to guide you. We'll identify a lead generation method that will more than double your sales leads. Are you ready for that?"

"I sure am," Jo-Anne replied.

Sally's notes

<u>Method: how to win</u>

Macro and micro-behaviour

We need to describe the behaviours we want team members to use at two levels:

Macro-behaviour = A broad description of the behaviour. e.g. asking a problem question.

Micro-behaviour = A specific description of what people need to do or say to achieve high performance. e.g. asking "if you had a house fire without adequate insurance cover for your belongings, what difficulties would you face?"

How we can identify the high-performance behaviours

- Review our existing training materials
- Observe and interview our high performers
- Interview managers of our high-performing teams
- Find out what best practice is

CHAPTER 8

DEVELOPING
THE METHOD

Behaviours for lead generation

"Lead generation is a form of cross-selling," James said. "There's a lot of sales experience between the four of us, so let's work out the macro-behaviours for lead generation."

He suggested the easiest way to explore this would be to use a retail example. The inner city park bordered a four-lane city street. Retail stores lined the opposite pavement. James led the group to the nearby intersection, across the street and down to the wide doorway of a bookstore. There was lotto signage in the window.

Bestselling fiction filled the front of the store, with cookbooks on the left wall and magazines down the back. They walked over to the lottery area. Mounted on the wall behind the counter was a large screen advertising the evening draw.

"Since its Wednesday, there's a lotto draw tonight," James said. "Players are coming in to buy their tickets.

For the retailer, there's an opportunity to sell other products. What's one of them?"

Sally looked at the counter display. There were many shiny scratch-it cards for sale. "They could up-sell to more expensive lotto tickets, or cross-sell scratch-it tickets."

James nodded. "The sales method is the same either way. Let's concentrate on cross-selling scratch-it tickets. If you were serving customers, when would be the right time to attempt the cross-sell?"

Triggers

Jo-Anne spoke up. "It's just like the inbound service calls we receive. The best time is after the agent has taken care of the customer's request. When it comes to the scratch-it, the best time is probably when the lotto ticket is printing."

"Agreed. The trigger to cross-sell is the printing of the lotto ticket. You'll need to identify the trigger for attempting to generate a Funeral Cover lead."

Jo-Anne removed a tablet from her handbag and started taking notes.

"Now you're prompted to start the cross-selling conversation, what would you say?"

"Would you like a scratch-it as well?" Sally said.

"That's the typical approach," James said. "But it's the wrong one if you want to maximise your sales conversion rate. If you were the customer, what would your reaction be to that question?"

She paused and thought about it for a few seconds. "I'd say no," she said. "I'd feel the salesperson didn't care about me, only about selling something."

While they were talking, a middle-aged woman walked into the store and up to the lotto counter. She looked at the screen behind the counter for a moment and then asked for a Powerball ticket.

James glanced briefly at the customer and then continued: "Let's explore a better way to handle the cross-sell. Imagine one of the scratch-it cards came out a week ago. Ten prizes of $25,000 are available. Each ticket costs three dollars. How could you easily draw the customer's attention to it?"

Mark said, "You could casually gesture to it and say, 'You might have noticed our latest scratch-it card'."

"I like it. You've already covered the first two macro-behaviours of the cross-selling method. You used a lead-in statement with 'You might have noticed'. Then you followed up with a product statement; in this case, 'our latest scratch-it card'. Notice we haven't asked a question yet. What's next?"

Jo-Anne looked at her tablet. So far she'd written:

- trigger

- lead-in statement

- product statement.

"I need to know what's in it for me," Jo-Anne said.

"Which is what?"

"There are ten prizes of $25,000 up for grabs."

James asked what that meant to her.

"It means I could win $25,000."

Feature–benefit statements

"Perfect. So we need to put all this information into a feature–benefit statement – that's the next macro-behaviour. But before we do, what's a feature?"

This time Mark responded by saying it was a specific fact about a product. In this case, the scratch-it card had only just become available with ten prizes of $25,000.

"And what's a benefit of a product?"

"It's what it can do for you. In this case, the customer could win $25,000."

The woman who'd bought the Powerball ticket walked past their group as she left the store. "Good luck," Sally said to her. "I hope that's the winning ticket." The woman's face lit up at the thought.

James smiled at Sally and then replied to Mark: "You're right, Mark. So the conversation could go like this. 'By the way, you might have noticed our latest scratch-it card. Ten prizes worth $25,000 are available to win, which means you could be a lucky $25,000 winner today.'"

"That's a compelling offer," Sally said. "Especially if it's only going to cost me three dollars."

"Great. Now, we just need to ask a commitment question. That's the final macro-behaviour in the cross-selling method. In this case, we'd be asking for the sale because it's a small cost, so you might say, 'Would you like one?'"

Jo-Anne's notes now read:

- trigger

- lead-in statement

- product statement

- feature–benefit statement

- commitment question.

She started to shift her weight from one foot to the other.

"Can we apply this to lead generation for Funeral Cover now?" she asked.

"Sure. Let's find somewhere more private to do that."

James led them to the back of the store away from the other customers. There were travel guides on one side of the aisle and boating and motorcycling magazines on the other. They could talk here without being overheard.

"Jo-Anne, what's the trigger, and what are the lead-in and product statements your team could use?"

"I think the trigger should be when the agent completes the customer request. They could say something like, 'Just while you're on the line, I should quickly mention our Funeral Cover.'"

"Makes sense. Let's think about the feature–benefit statement. Often there'll only be one or two real benefits of interest to potential customers. What's the most compelling feature of your policy?"

"We make a cash payment within forty-eight hours of the claim."

James asked what benefit this provided to customers.

"They'll have peace of mind knowing their loved ones won't have any financial concerns at a time when they're grieving."

The opening of the stockroom door at the end of the aisle interrupted their discussion. A college-aged girl wearing the store's black uniform with bright green accents emerged. Seeing the four of them standing there, she asked if they needed any help. When Sally told her they didn't, she went over to talk with the sales assistant on the counter.

James picked up the conversation again. "So the feature–benefit statement might go something like this: 'We make a cash payment within forty-eight hours of the claim. Which means you get peace of mind knowing your loved ones won't have any financial concerns at a time when they're grieving.'"

Jo-Anne smiled. "I like that. The customer service agent could then finish with a commitment question. Perhaps, 'Would you like to find out more?' If the customer's interested, we'll have a lead for one of Mark's sales agents to follow up."

"Exactly," James said. "Of course, some of your agents may want to adjust the words, to make it more natural for them. What's important is they stick with the order of the macro-behaviours. Which are: lead-in statement, product statement, feature–benefit statement and commitment question. I suggest you experiment with feature–benefit statements. Get your agents to track their lead conversion rates. That will help you identify the highest converting statement."

"I can get started with my teams this afternoon," Jo-Anne said. "We'll brainstorm the phrases people can try, and have a think about other feature–benefit statements we should test. If we get the testing underway tomorrow, we'll have useful data by the end of next week."

"Thanks for your help today, James," Mark said. "You've given us lots of good ideas. I'll get my team started this afternoon." Sally and Jo-Anne also thanked James. They said they'd be back in touch sometime the following week. They all shook hands with James.

"I look forward to it," he said.

Sally's notes

Example of a method: lead generation for Funeral Cover

To be used by our inbound agents once they've taken care of the customer's request.

Macro-behaviour	Micro-behaviour examples
1. Lead-in statement	"While you're on the line … "
2. Product statement	"… I should quickly mention our Funeral Cover."
3. Feature–benefit statement	"We make a cash payment within forty-eight hours of the claim. Which means you get peace of mind knowing your loved ones won't have any financial concerns at a time when they're grieving."
4. Commitment question	"Would you like to find out more?"

CHAPTER 9

A COACHING LESSON

Progress report

Thursday morning the following week, Sally was heading back to her office with a latte in hand. Coming out of the lift, she put her head down as she walked past Doyle's office. But because of the glass panels, he could see people walking by.

"Sally," he called out.

She did not want to talk to Doyle right now, or tomorrow come to think of it. Even so, she forced a smile as she turned to acknowledge him.

He waved her in. "Come in. How are things?"

Doyle occupied a large, well-appointed corner office. Sally reckoned it had enough space to host a good-sized Friday drinks party. Not that anyone would want to come. She noticed some of the furnishings – such as the desk and sideboard – were unique to this room. They were dark, wooden and masculine.

Sally told him what Mark's outbound centre managers had been doing. They'd worked out how to increase conversions of Fairweather and Funeral Cover products. She also said that all the agents in Jo-Anne's inbound teams were now using a script to generate Funeral Cover leads.

That got a smug look from Doyle. "It's about time. But, what's this about a script?"

Sally felt her palms become damp. She told him about the lead generation approach James had shared. Doyle's eyes narrowed. "Are you sure you know what you're doing? I don't want our people sounding like robots."

It didn't seem to matter what she did: Doyle was always dubious about how successful it would be. He continued: "I'll tell you what … you get Jo-Anne to try this approach out, and come back and tell me when it goes … " He stopped before he finished the sentence. He turned and looked out the window.

"Give me an update on Monday," he finished abruptly, not turning back to face Sally.

She left Doyle's office hot with anger. Doyle had previously told her that he only cared about the numbers. *Well, he's right about that*, Sally thought. Catching herself, it occurred to her he might be worried about tomorrow's board meeting.

Back at her desk, she took several deep breaths. If she didn't get sales sorted out soon, not only was she going to continue having problems with Doyle, she was also going to have problems in her own marriage with all the late nights she was spending at work. It was time to call James again. The phone seemed to ring for a long time before he answered.

"Hey Sally, how're things?"

"Good and bad," she said. After getting the conversation with Doyle off her chest, she went on to talk about better news. This morning she'd watched teams celebrating as they updated their new scoreboards. There was more laughter than usual. Performance was moving up, but was still nowhere close to their target.

"Don't worry. It'll get there."

"Well, it needs to before Doyle gets any worse," Sally said. "You told me there are five things I need to understand to put a High-Performance Coaching system in place:

- what game we're playing

- how to win

- how to coach

- when to coach

- the need to referee the game.

Thanks to you we understand what game we're playing and how to win it. What I now need to understand is how to coach."

"Then let's organise a time to talk. I'm not available today, but I can come by your office tomorrow at midday."

"Thanks. I appreciate your help. I'll see you tomorrow."

How to coach

The following day, Sally was talking with one of the receptionists when James walked out of the lift. Dressed more smartly than usual, he was wearing a light blue checked shirt and a navy blazer. "Thanks for coming," she said. "Do you mind if we go to our cafeteria so I can eat while we talk?"

"Fine with me. I ate before I came," James said. He mentioned there were a few things he wanted to cover today, so he hoped she had enough time. Sally said she was free for as long as needed.

They walked down a flight of stairs and through to the cafeteria. There were only a few people scattered around the tables. Some were seated together talking over lunch, while others had a book or newspaper in front of them and were keeping to themselves. Sally carried a soft cooler bag with her. She led the way to a spare table next to a blank whiteboard.

James waited as Sally removed her lunch from the bag. She opened a container filled with salad and poured dressing over it from a small bottle.

James began: "To be able to coach for high performance, you need to be competent in several skills, including being able to specify behaviour and ask open-ended questions. You also need to be able to put those skills into use in six different coaching techniques."

"Six? Why so many? We only learnt one technique at the recent coaching course," said Sally.

"Coaching is situational. You need different approaches depending on what you're trying to achieve."

Sally asked what this meant.

James stood and took a black marker from the whiteboard behind them. Sally moved her chair to face it as he began to draw.

High-Performance Coaching techniques

Approach

Reinforce   Correct   Guide

Purpose

"There are three purposes to having a coaching conversation, and two different approaches for each," James said as he drew. "So, we have six different techniques all together." James then grabbed a blue marker and wrote the word 'purpose'.

The three purposes

He pointed to the word, 'reinforce'. "This is the first purpose. Think about the macro- and micro-behaviours you need your customer service agents to use; for example, using a specific feature–benefit statement when attempting to generate leads. You'll want to recognise your agents for using that behaviour in order to motivate them to keep doing it."

Then James pointed to the word 'correct': "If a person isn't using the required behaviour, or is off track in some way, you need to *correct* their behaviour."

Three young men came into the cafeteria, talking spiritedly about their gym workouts. Their conversation suggested that deadlifts were essential in any workout routine.

Pointing to the word 'guide', James continued: "On other occasions, you'll want to *guide* your agents on how to do their job better. Like helping them identify a specific action they can take to achieve the outcome they're seeking."

Between mouthfuls of salad, Sally had taken out her small red notebook and was making notes. "*Reinforce, correct* and *guide*. Makes sense," she said. "I now see the reason for all the confusion over what the word 'coaching' actually means. When some people use it, they mean guiding someone. Other people mean correcting behaviour. Not many people use it to mean reinforcing behaviour."

"Yet using informal, immediate and specific positive feedback to reinforce behaviour is the single most powerful way to increase employee performance."

The two approaches

Gesturing at the diagram, James continued, "And there are two ways you can achieve these outcomes – by *asking* and by *telling*." He added these approaches on the left side of the diagram.

High-Performance Coaching techniques

Ask			
Tell			
	Reinforce	Correct	Guide

Approach

Purpose

Sally frowned. She said that wasn't what they'd learnt at the coaching workshop. The facilitator had told them good coaching involves asking rather than telling.

"That's fine for life coaches, executive coaches and counsellors. Their job is to help people discover their answers. You can only do that by asking. But it's not enough when you're coaching for high performance. Imagine you were the coach of a high-level soccer team. What's the chance you'd only *ask* your players what they could do to improve?"

Sally dabbed her mouth with a napkin. "I see your point. You'd sometimes use that approach, but you'd also need to tell them what they're doing well."

James said that was right. He pointed to the top right corner of his diagram: "From what you've said, I suspect your recent coaching skills workshop only trained your managers to *guide* people by *asking* questions."

Sally thought for a second and then confirmed his assumption was correct.

"That means your managers only know one of the six coaching techniques. They're like carpenters who only have a hammer but no other tools. They'll treat everything as if it were a nail."

"So, then, what are the six coaching techniques?"

Sally's notes

Coaching is situational. We need different approaches depending on what we're trying to achieve.

3 reasons for coaching:

To reinforce behaviour

To correct behaviour

To guide behaviour

2 approaches for each:

Ask

Tell

CHAPTER 10

THE SIX HIGH-PERFORMANCE COACHING TECHNIQUES

High-Performance Coaching

James turned back to the whiteboard and filled in the six high-performing coaching techniques in red.

	Reinforce	Correct	Guide
Ask	Performance debrief	Corrective feedback	Guide conversation
Tell	Positive feedback	Impact message	Skills coaching

Approach

Purpose

Positive feedback and performance debrief (reinforcing)

He explained, "The first coaching technique is providing *positive feedback*. Managers will normally do this when they've noticed something a team member has done well. However, people sometimes achieve performance outcomes without you seeing what they did, in which case you can still provide coaching by doing a *performance debrief*." James pointed to the relevant section in his diagram as he talked.

Sally said, "That's especially important for managers like Jo-Anne and Mark. They can't see what their managers and team leaders are doing every day."

"That's true. But it's still just as important for them. They're often busy with other things and don't always notice the good work that's happening. They need a way to debrief what their people have been doing. From there they can identify what they can provide positive feedback about."

Sally nodded, her mouth full with the last of her salad.

Impact message and corrective feedback (correcting)

Moving on, James said, "When it comes to correcting behaviour, most managers make one of two mistakes: they either jump in too early or leave it too long."

"Too early?" Sally asked.

"Good people have bad days. There's no point spending time correcting someone who is going to self-correct anyway."

To illustrate this point, James asked Sally if she thought she was a good driver. She said she did. Then he asked her if she'd ever made a mistake at an intersection that had the potential to cause an accident. She confirmed she had.

James said, "So it's not whether someone makes a mistake that's important. It's whether there's a pattern of problem behaviour. Once you notice a trend in the problem behaviour, you'll want to take action. If you've noticed just a couple of instances of the problem behaviour, you can use an *impact message*. If there's a clear trend developing, you'd have a more in-depth *corrective feedback* conversation."

Sally held up her hand, signalling for James to pause while she made notes in her notebook. When she finished, she said, "You said some managers leave it too long to correct behaviour. Tell me more about that."

James explained that no-one was perfect. Once people started towards a goal, it was almost inevitable they'd go off track at some point. It happened with personal goals such as losing weight. It also occurred with work goals such as increasing conversion rates.

"Most team leaders don't know how to correct behaviour constructively," James explained. "As a result, some don't feel confident enough to take corrective action at the right time. Often that's because they don't want to come across as confrontational. So the problem behaviour becomes established and therefore more difficult to deal with."

Sally admitted she'd seen this happen many times throughout her career. A person's performance would drop and human resources would eventually be called in. The whole situation became complicated and time consuming.

Nine times out of ten things got out of hand because the team leader failed to take action early.

"James, before you take me through the last two coaching techniques, I'm going to grab a coffee. Do you want one as well?" Noticing him hesitate, she said, "Don't worry, we have a coffee machine. You can have the real thing."

He grimaced and confessed his dislike of instant coffee while Sally led him through to the kitchen area. A commercial-looking coffee machine clad in brushed aluminium sat proudly on the bench. Next to it was a large bowl filled with coffee capsules of different colours. Once James had made his choice, Sally prepared a cup of coffee for each of them. Then they returned to their table to continue their discussion.

Skills coaching and guide conversation (guiding)

"As you can see, the last two coaching techniques are for guiding team members," James said. "*Skills coaching* is a method for observational coaching. Originally developed for sports coaching, it's also effective for coaching sales, service and productivity behaviours. I've been using it for the past twenty years to help sales and service teams grow their performance."

"Do you mean observing live customer interactions and then coaching the team member between calls?" asked Sally.

"That's right. Team leaders can use it anytime they're observing one of their agents handling a customer call.

But centre managers can also use it when they're coaching a team leader who is coaching their agents."

"Perfect. That leaves us with the '*guide conversation*'. What's that?"

"It's a technique for guiding people to decide on the solutions to their problems themselves."

Sally consulted what she'd written in her small notebook. She tapped her pen on the table, as she sometimes did when she was thinking. When she looked up at James, she said, "This is the first time I've seen a clear description of the coaching techniques we need to use."

At that moment Sally's mobile rang. She glanced at the screen and let out a long, slow breath, saying she would have to take it. Answering the phone, Sally listened for a few seconds and told the caller she'd be right there. Turning to James, she said that Doyle needed to see her for a few minutes. She apologised and asked him to wait.

Sally returned 20 minutes later, ashen faced. "Doyle's just ripped into me, along with Trevor – he's the GM of Retail," she said. "There's a board meeting today, and they're unhappy with the slow progress we're making to lift revenue."

"Unhappy?" James reflected.

"Yeah. Doyle said if he didn't see major progress in the next month, our jobs were on the line. He's obviously overreacting, but still … " She paused and glanced at her unfinished coffee. "I could do with something stronger, but I'll settle for more caffeine."

Quick wins

Returning with her replacement coffee, Sally stared at the High–Performance Coaching techniques grid. "I don't have the time to train my leadership teams in six coaching techniques. I need to make progress immediately. Let's apply the 80/20 principle. What's the one we need to be using right now to get the biggest performance gains?"

"With Doyle pushing you so hard, you need to get some quick wins. Let's first look at the performance equation. It will help you identify the most essential High-Performance Coaching technique to get your team leaders using straight away," James said.

He returned to the whiteboard and wrote:

$$Performance = Effort \times Skill$$

He continued: "A person's performance depends on the effort they put into their job and their level of skill at doing it. Lack of effort is a major cause of performance problems. People often aren't motivated to take the action you need them to take. That's because their managers accidentally ignore most of their good work. Unfortunately, ignoring good work is nearly as destructive on a person's motivation as punishment for poor behaviour. It greatly reduces the amount of effort people are willing to put in."

Sally sat back in her chair and laid her hands on the table. "Motivation is what we've been struggling with. The low employee engagement scores reflect that," she said. "So to lift performance, our team leaders need to motivate their agents to use the high-performance behaviours."

She looked at the purposes James had drawn on the board. Sally said she presumed that reinforcing behaviour increased motivation the most. If you recognised people for what they were doing well, they were going to be more motivated to keep doing it. Correcting and guiding addressed what a person wasn't doing.

"That's insightful," James agreed.

"And providing positive feedback is the best way to do that?"

"Exactly right," James confirmed, as he stood again to circle those words in his diagram. "It also motivates them to self-correct when they're off track, without being told."

High-Performance Coaching techniques

	Reinforce	Correct	Guide
Ask	Performance debrief	Corrective feedback	Guide conversation
Tell	Positive feedback	Impact message	Skills coaching

Approach — Purpose

More people were now drifting into the cafeteria for lunch in groups of two or three. Most of them were young – in their twenties and early thirties. Almost all carried food they'd just purchased. Gourmet burgers, noodle boxes and sushi seemed to be on the menu today. Noticing the dress standard for men was chinos or dark jeans with a jacket, James felt like he fitted right in.

"Long term, you'll also need to pay attention to the other five coaching techniques," he said. "However, *positive feedback* is the most powerful High-Performance Coaching technique to motivate your people and maximise their performance."

Recognising and rewarding behaviour

"What about pay? I always thought that was important to motivation. After all, if someone's paid well to do their job, they should do their job well."

"Pay affects recruitment and retention, but not performance. People don't perform better when they're satisfied with the pay they're receiving. But they do start looking at other options when they're dissatisfied."

"I accept that," Sally said. "I was thinking more of using incentives to motivate agents to boost sales performance."

"There is a way to make incentives work extremely well, but you need to be careful of the disadvantages," James said.

"Such as?"

"For one, they can encourage dishonesty. You'll remember Mark mentioned the problem of incentives driving unethical sales behaviour at the last company he worked at. For another, they encourage short-term thinking."

Sally looked confused, so James continued.

"Incentives can encourage agents to make one-off sales, rather than sales that benefit the customer in the long term. They can also encourage agents to provide poor service to customers with more complex needs. By shortening the call, they can get onto their next sales opportunity."

"Okay, I get it," Sally said. "When you focus only on rewarding results, there's a chance you'll encourage behaviour you don't want. We've seen that with recent investigations into financial services misconduct. Some firms have been found to have pursued short-term profit at the expense of basic standards of honesty."

James said: "To keep people on track, your team leaders need to reinforce their agents' use of the behaviours you want. They can do that best by giving positive feedback. With that and the other parts of High-Performance Coaching in place, you'll boost performance in your objectives. Once you have those gains, you can then consider whether it would be helpful to use incentives. Doing it the other way around would be like building a house on sand. You won't have the foundation you need to get the sustainable improvements you want ethically."

Sally looked down and shook her head. "The crazy thing is I already know people respond well to recognition.

I'm a parent, after all. You can't raise great kids without providing lots of positive feedback. And I remember reading somewhere that employees who receive recognition are almost three times more engaged than those who don't. I don't understand why I haven't focused more on recognising people for what they've been doing well."

"It's because our brains are wired to notice negative things more than positive," James said.

"How do you mean?"

Negativity bias

James used his foot against a chair leg to turn it around. He sat down again, facing Sally over the back of the chair.

"Imagine you're asked to do a 20-minute presentation to the board. It goes extremely well, except you say just *one thing* you wish you hadn't. What do you think about for the rest of the day? All the things you did well in the presentation, or the one thing you wish you hadn't said?"

"The one thing I wish I hadn't said."

"That's your negativity bias in action. It means managers mostly focus on what people need to improve, not on what they're doing well. Your managers might know it's important to provide positive feedback, yet their brains are telling them about all the problems they need to fix. So they attend to the problems and ignore what their people are doing well."

Sally said: "And if all I hear about is how poorly I'm doing, I'm going to become demotivated. To come back to a point Jo-Anne made the other day, I'll feel like I'm being micro-managed. My performance will drop as well as my engagement." Her lips tightened. "Now I see our problem. My centre managers and team leaders have to stop ignoring what their people are doing well. They have to start catching their people doing things *right*."

"Exactly," James said.

Sally's notes

To reinforce behaviour

- Positive Feedback is the best way to motivate team members to use the high-performance behaviours.

- The Performance Debrief helps a manager uncover details of behaviour they haven't seen, so they can give positive feedback.

To correct behaviour

- Use the Impact Message if there are a couple of instances of off-track behaviour.

- Give Corrective Feedback if a trend in problem behaviour has developed.

To guide behaviour

- Skills Coaching is for observational/side-by-side coaching.

- The Guide Conversation helps a team member identify the solution to a problem they have.

CHAPTER 11

PROVIDING POSITIVE FEEDBACK

The importance of positive feedback

At that moment, Jo-Anne entered the cafeteria with a tall, strong-looking man in his mid-thirties. Sporting a large beard and a linen jacket, he wore his hair short on the sides and longer on top.

Sally waved them over and invited them to join the conversation. They made themselves a drink first, and then Jo-Anne introduced the man to James. His name was Nick, and he was one of her centre managers.

"Good to meet you," Nick said to James. "Jo-Anne's been telling me about her discussions with you."

Sally recapped what James had been sharing with her.

Nick nodded. "I understand the importance of positive feedback. But when I've provided it from time to time – such as in a monthly one-on-one – I can't say I've seen an increase in performance."

"Think of positive feedback like a leaking tap dripping water into a plugged sink," James said. "One drop of water doesn't even wet the bottom. But drop by drop, the sink slowly fills, and eventually it overflows. Likewise, one bit of positive feedback isn't going to change anyone's life. Yet, drop by drop, day by day, positive feedback motivates people to put in the effort to repeat what they're doing well and to start doing what they're not. It also creates a massive improvement in engagement."

"You're reminding me of a time when positive feedback did have a huge motivational effect on me," Nick said. "Back when I was an agent, the best team leader I worked for spent time most days watching me in action and listening to a few of my calls. He was always telling me how good I was. That did motivate me to do well."

"Your people are the same. Daily positive feedback can increase performance by a healthy margin. The best part is it's free, easy, and you can use it often without people tiring of it."

"You sound like an infomercial," Sally said with a smile.

"But wait … there's more!" he said. Heads turned as their laughter distracted others from their lunchtime conversations. "Positive feedback only takes a few seconds to give, so even the busiest manager has time to give it."

Nick glanced at his phone. "There's a meeting room in my contact centre that is available for the next hour. We could go down there, so we don't disturb people's lunchtimes any further."

"Good idea," said Sally.

How to give positive feedback

The meeting room had a light and airy feel, with a glass wall on one side that gave a view over Nick's contact centre. One of the side walls supported a large screen, and a whiteboard occupied the back wall. Sally sat at the back of the room facing towards the contact centre.

Once they'd settled in, Jo-Anne said, "We probably provide positive feedback without thinking about it. The thing is, I'm not sure of the best approach to take."

"Let me talk you through the approach I recommend," James said. He got up and wrote on the whiteboard.

How to give positive feedback

Give positive feedback immediately

Start with positive words

Describe one or two micro-behaviours

Describe the positive impact of the behaviour (optional)

Nick unlocked his phone and asked if he could take a photo. James encouraged him to do so. Jo-Anne removed her tablet from her handbag and powered it on, and Sally pulled out her notebook.

"The purpose of positive feedback is to reinforce a behaviour," James said. "You want to encourage the person to keep repeating it. If you reinforce the high-performance sales, service and productivity behaviours, performance will increase. Of course, people like recognition for their effort and good work, so they feel good as well."

While James talked, Sally studied the contact centre. The teams sat at large circular pods. Each pod had dividers separating them into eight individual workstations. And each team was spread across two pods, with the team leader at one of them. She could see where the team leaders sat because they each had a small red flag on top of their computer screen. It was a simple way to find them at a glance. She noticed all the team leaders were at their desks.

Giving positive feedback immediately

Nick laced his hands together behind his head and leaned back in his chair. "Why do we need to give positive feedback *immediately*? Why can't we wait until the team meeting or their next one-on-one?"

"Providing positive feedback only during those types of meetings isn't enough. You wouldn't get the performance and engagement gains you're seeking," James said. "You need to shift your thinking about coaching. It's something that needs to happen throughout each day, not just in meetings. I'd go as far as to say it's the day-to-day coaching conversations you have with your people that make the greatest difference to their performance."

"I still don't understand why delaying my positive feedback would make any difference."

"Imagine you bake a chocolate cake. You share it with your team in celebration of them exceeding their target for the month. Imagine further that no-one from the team thanked you for doing so at the time. But a week later, one of your team finally does so. They say it was thoughtful of you to bake a cake for the team in recognition of their efforts. What would your reaction be to this positive feedback?"

Nick sat up and scratched his beard. "It would have disappointed me that no-one said anything positive at the time about the effort I'd made. A positive comment a week later is far from heartfelt," he said. Sally and Jo-Anne murmured their agreement.

"How likely are you to do something similar again?" James asked.

"Unlikely."

James encouraged Nick to imagine a slightly different scenario. The same team member is one of several people who thanked him for his effort at the time of the celebration. She even dropped a note on his desk afterwards, which said, "Thanks for making the wonderful chocolate cake for us. Delicious!", followed by a smiley face. He wondered how Nick would respond.

"That feels much more sincere, and I'd feel good receiving that positive feedback. I'd be happy to bake another cake the next time the team exceeds their monthly target," said Nick.

"Yet the only thing that changed was *when* they thanked you. The longer you wait to provide positive feedback, the less it motivates someone to repeat the behaviour."

"Got it."

Starting with positive words

James pointed to the second point he'd written on the whiteboard. "Next, you need to start the conversation with positive words," he said. To demonstrate why that was important, he asked Jo-Anne if she'd be willing to help out. She nodded.

"Imagine I say to you, 'Have you got a moment Jo-Anne? I've got some feedback for you.' What's your reaction to that?"

Jo-Anne looked slightly worried. "I'm not expecting good news," she said.

"Even though I didn't say anything negative, you automatically assumed the worst. The absence of any positive words is enough for your negativity bias to kick in. So it's important to say something positive early on. I'm sure it would have felt better if I'd said, 'Hey, great news Jo-Anne. Have you got a moment? I've got some feedback for you.'"

Jo-Anne beamed. "Much better," she said as she swivelled back and forth in her chair.

Describing one or two micro-behaviours

James pointed to the third point: "The next step is to describe one or two micro-behaviours. Let's find one you might want to reinforce. Nick, what's an objective your team's focused on improving?"

"Agent availability."

"Terrific. I recall you've decided a key activity to improve availability is logging in before the rostered time. What micro-behaviour have you found makes the biggest difference?"

Nick scratched his beard again. "We're getting agents to ensure they're arriving at their work station one minute before they're rostered to start. That gives them enough time to get settled and log in, so they're ready to start on time."

"That's a perfect example. When giving positive feedback, you want to provide that level of detail. But it's important to only mention one or two micro-behaviours. Sally, why do you think that is?" James asked.

Sally was momentarily caught out. She was still watching the teams below. She'd noticed all the team leaders were still at their desks as if chained to their computers; a flash of annoyance had bubbled up in her, and she took a moment to regroup.

"You need them to know exactly why you are giving positive feedback," she said. "You want to encourage them to keep repeating the behaviour, so they need to know what they are doing well." Sally also thought it important to keep to only one or two behaviours as any more may be too many to remember.

"Exactly."

Describing the positive impact

She glanced at James from under a furrowed brow. "What's this optional extra?"

"Describing the positive impact of the person's behaviour acts like a supercharger on an engine. It makes your positive feedback more powerful. Helping people understand how their work positively impacts others gives what they do meaning. So, it's one of the most powerful drivers of employee engagement."

"That's no small thing."

"You're right, though it isn't strictly necessary. You'll be able to encourage people to repeat high-performance behaviour more frequently without mentioning the positive impact of that behaviour. However, your positive feedback will be even more powerful when you do mention it," James said.

Putting it all together

"Now let's put all the parts together. Imagine I'm a team leader, and Nick is one of my agents. I've checked the roster as I know some agents will be shortly coming back from break. I notice Nick arrives back at his work station about a minute or so before he's due to be available to customers."

Sally put her pen to paper, ready to take notes.

James continued: "And so I say, 'Thanks, Nick. I appreciate you making an effort to get back a minute before the end of your break. Your drive to log in on time is helping us reduce the time customers have to wait. Good work.'"

Nick was grinning.

"I know this is a fictional example, but how would you feel if this was a real situation?" James asked.

Nick said he felt good receiving positive feedback. If this were a real situation, he'd be happy. And his motivation to return to his work station a minute or so before the end of his break in the future would increase.

James turned to Jo-Anne. "How long did that conversation take?"

"No more than ten seconds."

"And given that Nick said he'd keep using this behaviour, what's the return on a team leader's time for giving positive feedback?"

"Huge. But I'm curious … what about a sales situation, such as an attempt at lead generation? What would you do if the customer wasn't interested, and Nick didn't get a lead?" Jo-Anne leaned forward, playing with the big beads of her necklace – green ones today. "Would you give him positive feedback in those circumstances?"

"No matter how good an agent is, they're not going to succeed on every attempt. You already know which macro- and micro-behaviours generate the most leads. You need to encourage them to keep using those behaviours, regardless of the outcome with any specific customer."

Jo-Anne nodded. "That makes sense. Still, it's going to take a mind shift for many of our team leaders, and even some of our centre managers."

Nick wanted to know how much positive feedback his team leaders should be providing to their agents. James suggested an excellent rule of thumb was to give positive feedback to average performing agents most days. Team members new to their role should get more, while high performers could get by with less.

"That's a lot more than we give now. Providing that much positive feedback may not seem very sincere to the people receiving it," Nick said.

"The purpose of this positive feedback is to help your people improve their performance," said James. "It's important your team leaders keep that in mind. However, there are two things they can do to come across as sincere when they're giving positive feedback. The first is to describe only one micro-behaviour the agent did well. That will keep it short and specific. The second is to describe the positive impact of the behaviour. That will give a clear reason for the positive feedback conversation. We've already discussed these."

"Good tips. Thanks," said Nick.

Sally continued to watch the team leaders. Still none of them had moved from their desks. Her brain raced. *How are they going to give that amount of positive feedback? They don't even get up and spend time with their agents.* Jo-Anne looked at her watch. It was time for Nick and her to go. They thanked James for his guidance, and Jo-Anne said she was sure they'd make more progress now.

"We've got a problem"

Once Jo-Anne and Nick had left, Sally said, "We've got a problem."

"What's that?" asked James.

"Take a look at the team leaders. They're the people with the small red flags on top of their screens. What do you notice them doing?"

James walked to the glass and looked out. All but one of the pods was filled with people sitting at their workstations wearing headphones. The empty pod had a banner over it with the words 'Knight Riders' – probably belonging to the evening team. A lone agent walked back to her workstation, mug in hand. Apart from her, there was no-one walking around the centre.

He said, "They're sitting at their desks rather than coaching their teams."

"What do you suggest we do about that?"

"It's a problem, I agree. But, let's deal with that later. Your centre managers and team leaders first need to understand the importance of positive feedback and how to give it. If we don't attend to that at the outset, your team leaders will give more correction than positive feedback in their coaching. The opposite of what you need to lift performance."

Sally's notes

How to give positive feedback

- Give positive feedback immediately
- Start with positive words
- Describe one or two micro-behaviours
- Describe the positive impact of the behaviour (optional)

Daily positive feedback motivates people to put in the effort to repeat what they're doing well and to start doing what they need to.

To lift their performance, average performing agents need positive feedback most days for their use of high-performance behaviour. Team members new to their role need more, and high performers require less.

CHAPTER 12

FINDING THE RHYTHM

Struggling

Sally paced back and forth in her office to reduce her anxiety. It was one way to work towards her 10,000 steps a day, but not one she was enjoying.

Twelve days had passed since she'd last spoken with James. Performance across her service and sales centres was improving. But it was happening far too slowly for her liking. She wondered if her teams were ever going to hit their targets. In his emails, Doyle had made it clear he didn't think so.

Moreover, she wasn't sure she wanted to continue at Velocity. It wasn't her fault sales had declined before she'd started. Earlier in the week she'd received a message from an executive recruiter. He was looking for someone with her level of contact centre experience to place in a well-regarded company across town. She'd had a call with him, and what the company was offering sounded good. She would only have to maintain performance there, not transform it. Their CEO was known to have built a positive culture, so there would be no more dealing with people like Doyle.

She sighed, knowing it was the stress and guilt making her think like this. There was the pressure from failing to meet expectations at work. There was also the guilt of not spending enough time with her family.

They had made some progress, though. Jo-Anne and Mark had trained all the centre managers and team leaders by video conference, so they all knew how to give positive feedback and how often to provide it. Most had been keen to get started, and there were already reports of improved morale. But it wasn't making as much difference to overall performance as she'd have liked.

Most of Sally's contact centres were in other towns and cities. To get an idea of how things were going, she'd visited the inbound and outbound centres in her building that morning. And she was not happy with what she saw. It was plain to see the contact centre managers weren't spending time coaching their team leaders, nor were the team leaders coaching their agents. All they seemed to do was sit at their computers.

She looked out the window at the park below and sighed. *Some fresh air would be good*, she thought.

When to coach

Out walking in the park, Sally felt the crunch of the gravel path under her feet. With a clearer head, the next piece of the High-Performance Coaching system came to mind – when to coach.

At that moment a voice called out: "Hey, Sally!" It was James, striding along the path towards her.

"Hi James, what are you doing here?"

"I was in the area and thought I'd check if you were free, so it's great to run into you. How about you?"

Sally dropped her shoulders. "Getting some fresh air to try to figure out what to do next."

"It doesn't sound like you're in a good place." He gestured over his shoulder. "There's a park bench just down the path there. Let's sit and talk."

The bench was in the shade, overlooking the university soccer pitch. A student team dressed in a light blue strip was practising. Several players wore yellow bibs to distinguish them from the others. A young woman carrying a whistle ran around the field with them. It looked to Sally like she was the coach.

Getting amongst it

"What's been going on?" James asked, resting his elbows on the back of the bench.

"Progress on lifting our performance is slower than I'd like. All the centre managers and team leaders know how to give positive feedback now. They're also clear on my expectations of how frequently to provide it. I hear good things about the impact it's having on morale and individual performance. But I'm troubled by what I saw in our local centres this morning. The centre managers and team leaders appeared to be chained to their desks, like last week. I can't see how we're going to improve any further if that continues."

James nodded. "It's a common problem that holds back performance in many companies … Look at the soccer team out there. Where's the coach?"

"Out on the ground coaching her players," Sally replied. James pointed out that sports coaches spend most of their coaching time on the field. They didn't spend it on a computer or in a meeting room.

Sally gripped the edge of the bench. "That's the exact opposite of what my managers and team leaders are doing. They're spending virtually no time at all on the floor with their teams."

James said her centre managers and team leaders had to act more like sports coaches and less like administrators. She could achieve this by specifying the coaching rhythm she needed them to follow, and then holding them accountable for doing so.

Sally frowned. "What's 'coaching rhythm'?"

Two young women jogged by, talking about a movie one of them had seen. "That's my term for the cycle of meetings you expect your managers to have with their team members in which they communicate, coach and hold them accountable," James said to Sally.

"I've heard colleagues in other companies talk about operating rhythm. Is that the same thing?"

"Yes, some industries do use that term. Your managers know *what* to coach. You've figured that out with the ROAM model. They now know *how* to provide positive feedback to reinforce behaviour. We can train them in the other five coaching techniques shortly. The biggest thing they're now missing is *when* to coach, which is where coaching rhythm comes in."

He went on to explain it was crucial for managers to have a planned rhythm of formal meetings and informal interactions. Some daily, others weekly, fortnightly and monthly.

"What sort of meetings do you have in mind?" Sally asked.

"Well, here's something I prepared earlier," James said with a smile. He leaned forward, pulled a rectangle of paper from his hip pocket and unfolded it.

Coaching Rhythm

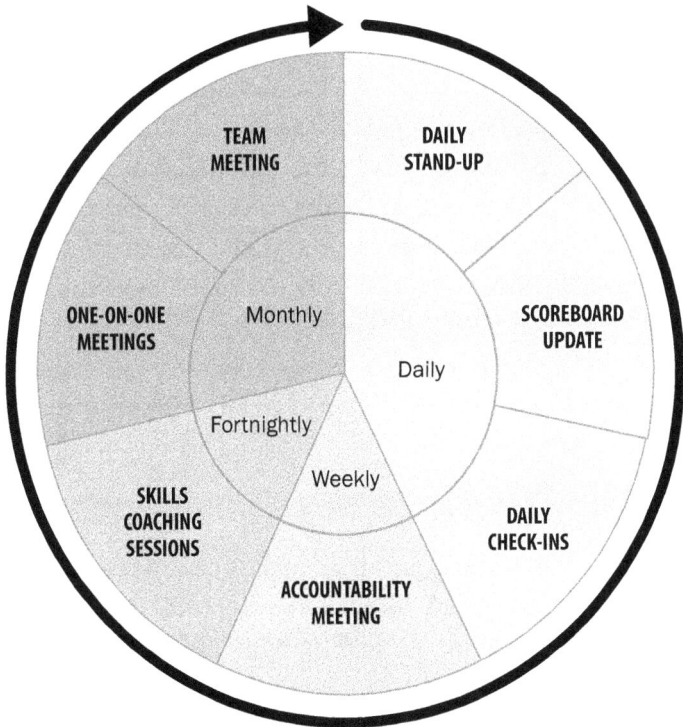

"This is what best-practice coaching rhythm looks like in my experience."

James placed the diagram on his knee and traced around it with his right index finger. "The daily stand-up, weekly accountability meeting and monthly team meeting are all activities with the team. Managers do the other activities with individual team members – such as Skills Coaching, which some people call side-by-side coaching."

Sally said nothing for a few seconds while she studied the diagram. She then leaned over and tapped the top of the page.

Getting together

"I've seen daily stand-ups work well," she said. "They can be a very motivating way to start the day. They'd be the perfect time to update the scoreboards. Our centre managers and outbound team leaders will be able to run them successfully. But, the rosters might prevent our inbound team leaders from running them."

"It's certainly more challenging running daily stand-ups with inbound teams," James agreed. "However, you'll want all your teams to have time for a weekly accountability meeting."

"What's that?"

"It's a short team meeting held once a week instead of a daily stand-up. It provides an opportunity to hold team members accountable for progress on their enabling objectives. And at least once a month, a longer team meeting should replace it. That allows time to do things like training and discussing issues unrelated to performance."

"Well, fortnightly team meetings are business as usual because we have to roster for them, though I don't know what happens in them. We also now have scoreboards in place, as you know. One-on-ones should be happening, but I can't put my hand on heart and say they are. The same can be said about skills coaching, unfortunately."

The sound of a whistle from the soccer field caught their attention. One of the players had scored. Two of his teammates slapped him on the shoulder in acknowledgement while he fist-bumped another.

Sally's notes

Coaching rhythm: when to coach

What our team leaders and centre managers need to be doing:

Daily: Stand-up

                  Scoreboard update

                  Check-ins

Weekly: Accountability Meeting

Fortnightly: Skills coaching sessions

Monthly: One-on-one meetings

                  Team meeting

CHAPTER 13

THE MISSING COACHING ACTIVITIES

"There are two parts of coaching rhythm you don't have yet that you need to get in place right now. In combination with scoreboards, they'll make the biggest difference to performance."

"I know what one of them is," Sally sighed. "They should be out on the floor coaching their people throughout the day. Is that what's referred to as 'daily check-ins' on your diagram?"

Daily check-ins

James nodded. "Sure is. There's a reason your performance is only growing slowly at the moment. Your team leaders aren't providing enough positive feedback to their agents. That's because they don't have a way of finding opportunities to provide it."

He explained that check-ins consist of short daily coaching interactions with team members. They allowed team leaders and managers to observe and coach their people while they work, and to carry out performance debriefs. That way, team leaders could notice trends in agent behaviour and seek opportunities to provide positive feedback to reinforce behaviour. As well as provide support to help agents find solutions to their problems.

"So it's like ... management by wandering around?"

"Daily check-ins aren't about wandering around. They're about deliberately paying attention to what people are doing. The most important reason for doing them is to find good work to provide positive feedback on. However, one challenge your managers will face is their negativity bias."

Sally's lips tightened. She looked grim. "You mean they'll look for what people are doing *wrong*, rather than what they're doing *right*."

James nodded. He said this caused problems because negatives had a greater impact on a person's psychological state than positives – even when they were of equal intensity. Negatives stuck like glue in people's minds, while positives slipped off and disappeared. So while correction was easily remembered, positive feedback was not. But there was an easy way to overcome this problem. Sally's centre managers and team leaders needed to give much more positive feedback than corrective.

"How much more?"

"At least five times more positive than corrective across the team seems to be the sweet spot," James replied.

"Wow! That's a lot. Are you sure that much positive feedback is necessary?"

"You'll be able to tell me in a minute. Imagine a situation in which you've reported to me for several months. You notice I provide lots of positive feedback, though I'm also willing to correct your behaviour when necessary. Let's say the feedback ends up around five positive feedback conversations for every corrective. How are you going to feel in most of our interactions?"

Sally smiled. "Since you provide so much positive feedback, I'd probably trust you and feel motivated by your comments. I'd also feel like I was doing a good job, and I could get the support I needed from you."

"That being the case, what would be your likely reaction to any positive feedback I gave you?" James asked.

"I'd feel good, and I'd keep repeating the behaviour you recognised. Of course, that's what you want."

"And what would be your likely reaction to the occasional corrective feedback conversation I had with you?"

Sally thought about it. In the distance, she could hear the coach on the soccer pitch yelling positive feedback to one of her players. "I'd think you intended to help me improve. So I'd regard it as good coaching and take action on whatever I agreed to do. You know, what I find interesting is that I'd probably regard it as a positive conversation rather than a negative one."

She could again hear the coach calling out praise for something done well by one of the players. James's questions and the actions of the soccer coach allowed Sally a flash of insight: "You're right. If we want to beat our targets, we need to be reaching for that five-to-one ratio of positive feedback to corrective. Our centre managers and team leaders need to be out doing check-ins with their team members each day. That will allow them to provide positive feedback for what their team members are doing well."

Sally wanted to know the numbers. How many check-ins should her managers do each day? James told her team leaders needed to do enough check-ins to ensure average performing agents got positive feedback most days, while those new to their role got it up to twice daily. Check-ins with high performers could happen less often but were still needed throughout the week. Centre managers should follow the same frequencies with their team leaders.

"Here's what I can tell you based on more than two decades of experience," James said. "The more check-ins your team leaders do each day, the higher their team performance will be. And your centre managers will influence that by the number of check-ins they do with their team leaders."

Feeling a sense of urgency, Sally bounced to her feet and said, "I need to get started on this straight away."

"Not so fast," James cautioned with a smile. "I said there are *two* parts of coaching rhythm you don't have that you need to get in place right now. The process of doing daily check-ins is only one of them."

Sally's shoulders slumped slightly.

"Come on. Let's walk," suggested James. "How about we take a turn around the soccer field?" Without waiting for a response, he stood abruptly and sped off. When Sally finally caught up, half running to do so, he slowed so she could fall into step beside him.

James continued: "Don't worry. It'll be well worth the effort addressing this next component of coaching rhythm. The primary purpose of daily check-ins is to find opportunities to reinforce high-performance behaviour. That's why they're so critical. Your scoreboards track performance, so every team knows how well they're playing the game. What's missing is — "

"A process for holding people accountable for taking action to improve their results," Sally interrupted.

Weekly accountability meeting

"The accountability meeting," he confirmed, then stopped walking as quickly as he'd started. Sally continued on for several steps before realising she'd left him behind. They were on the edge of the soccer pitch, and James was watching the players. Gesturing towards them, he said, "Notice how the coach is out on the field during practice, essentially doing check-ins. We've heard her giving positive feedback, but she'll also be providing correction and guidance where necessary. Her focus is to lock in the high-performance behaviours that are going to make these players successful."

Sally nodded, unsure of where James was taking this.

"During the match, everyone keeps their eye on the scoreboard. That tells them how well they are playing the game. When do you reckon she runs an accountability meeting?" he said.

Sally smiled broadly at James. "You have a way of making things seem so obvious. Clearly, she'll lead an accountability meeting at the start of the first practice session each week. I imagine they'd review the priority result – the score from the weekend's game. If they have data from video analysis, they'd also review performance on their enabling objectives. Those might be metrics like passes completed or goal assists."

"What else?"

"No doubt they'd discuss what happened to their performance, and what factors contributed. Teams are always going to learn from their successes and failures if they take time to do this."

"You're right of course. What else might the team do in the review?" James asked.

"Well, for many teams that might be it. But good coaches are probably going to have each team member commit to working on something specific to improve in their game. So they'd want to discuss who took action on what they committed to, and who didn't. There are always going to be some great coaching opportunities out of that. I can imagine the coach using several of the six coaching techniques."

Sally paused for a moment, lifting her head and staring into the distance. "Peer pressure is going to come into play as well," she continued. "Players won't want to let their teammates down."

James said, "Those steps would take up most of the accountability meeting. It's where most of the discussion, problem solving and coaching happens. Then, to finish up, it would be reasonable to expect each team member to commit to a specific activity or skill to work on over the coming week."

"Okay, I've got it," Sally said, tapping her head lightly. "Daily check-ins, scoreboard updates and weekly account-ability meetings are all non-negotiable."

Thanking him for his guidance, she said she'd be in touch and disappeared down the path at a brisk pace.

As Sally strode back to the office, her phone pinged. It was a message from the recruiter asking whether it was a good time to talk about that job offer. However, Sally's conversation with James had caused a change of heart. She'd never given up on a challenge yet. With the final pieces of the puzzle falling into place, she was not going to start now.

Back at her desk, she called the recruiter and left a message. She said a better opportunity had come up with a company that desperately needed her help to increase performance.

Sally's notes

The next parts of coaching rhythm to get in place

Daily check-ins:

- The daily activity of observing, debriefing and coaching people as they work.

- They provide an excellent opportunity to notice trends in behaviour and to give positive feedback and support.

- Leaders need to give their teams much more positive feedback than correction – at least five times as much.

- Team leaders must do enough check-ins for agents to get the right amount of positive feedback.

- Centre managers need to do the same with each of their team leaders.

Weekly accountability meeting:

- A weekly team meeting to review progress, hold people accountable for their activity and provide coaching.

- Review progress on the priority result and enabling objectives.

- Have team members report on their weekly commitment.

- Discuss the reasons for success and failure and provide coaching as required.

- Get a commitment from each team member for an action they'll take during the coming week to increase performance.

CHAPTER 14

GETTING VISIBILITY OF MANAGER ACTIVITY

Turning things around

Seven weeks later, Sally was in a much better place. The pressure was finally coming off with the performance improvements her teams were achieving. It was time to confront Doyle.

He had a surprised look on his face when she strode into his office.

"We need to talk," Sally said, closing his office door.

"What about?" he asked, looking back at his computer screen. He gestured towards the chair near his desk.

Sally decided to remain standing. She said: "Sales conversion for Fairweather and Funeral Cover combined is up by 17% from two months ago. We've also more than doubled our Funeral Cover leads. Those two improvements have made a huge difference in sales revenue, as you know. We've also increased agent availability in the service centres by 11%. That's helped us come close to achieving our grade of service target on most days. We hadn't been anywhere near that target for months. So, I want your support."

She was pleased to see she had his attention.

"My support?"

"Ever since I started here I've felt like you've wanted me to fail. All I've had from you is criticism. I know we're not hitting our targets yet, but I've stopped the decline in sales revenue and started growing it again. I know what I'm doing, and I deserve your support for what I've achieved in the past five months."

He looked at her for several long seconds. Then he seemed to come to a decision. "I respect you for having the courage to say that. You've put some good runs on the board, I agree, but there's one thing still bothering me. If you take action to address it, I'll back you. You have my word."

"What is it?"

"Come around here and take a look." He swivelled one of his two computer screens slightly for her to see.

Still work to do

She walked around the end of his desk and leant forward with both her hands on the desktop. As she did so, she noticed a black photo frame in front of her. To her surprise, it held a photograph of two boys with their arms around each other's shoulders. They appeared to be twins in their late teens. *There's a heart somewhere in there, after all*, thought Sally. Glancing up at the computer screen, she noticed it displayed a spreadsheet of performance for her division.

Doyle said, "Your centres have improved their sales performance, I'll give you that. However, the range of performance has become worse. You have one centre where performance hasn't improved at all. And in every centre that has improved, you have one or more teams whose performance hasn't changed."

Because the team leaders haven't been doing daily check-ins and giving positive feedback. And they probably haven't been running weekly accountability meetings either, Sally thought to herself.

He took Sally through all the sales reporting, centre by centre and team by team. She said he had a valid point. She'd also noticed those trends in the weekly reporting. They hadn't worried her at the time. Sales performance had been improving overall, and she'd had more pressing issues. She told him she would let him know Monday what she was doing about it.

"Thanks. You've done a good job so far."

Sally was taken aback. She didn't quite know how to handle the new Doyle, or at least the side of him she hadn't seen before. So she stammered out her thanks and left.

On the way back to her office, her phone rang.

"Hi James, how are you? What's that – how are things here? I'm thrilled with how we're getting on." She went on to tell him about the performance improvements they'd achieved. He said it was exciting to hear.

Sally continued, "Doyle's backing me for once, but it's not all perfect, unfortunately. I still have a huge concern about the lack of accountability. I'm certain many of our team leaders and centre managers still aren't doing as much coaching as we need." She could hear traffic in the background. "Are you in the city today?"

James said he was and could come by in about 45 minutes if she wanted.

"We'll make that work. See you then." She called Jo-Anne and Mark to ask them to meet with her immediately.

When James arrived at reception, Sally invited him up to her office.

Walking in, he found Jo-Anne and Mark seated around a circular meeting table. Sun poured into the far side of the office through the large windows. Even so, the air-conditioning kept the room at a comfortable temperature.

After getting a progress update from the pair, James asked about the concerns they and Sally had.

Mark leaned forward. "We haven't yet trained our managers in all of the High-Performance Coaching techniques. That leaves me feeling a little uneasy. Particularly given they don't know the best way to correct behaviour. But we're still achieving performance gains every week, so it's not our top priority."

"That's right," Jo-Anne chimed in. "We have a larger issue." She went on to outline the concerns they had over the variability in performance.

Sally held up her hands to command attention. "The thing that's bothering me the most is our complete lack of visibility about what's causing this. I remember a point you made when we first met on the golf course. You said that our team leaders hold the key to our success. Their coaching activity directly affects their teams' performance.

We've certainly found that to be true over the past few months."

Mark and Jo-Anne nodded in agreement.

"You also asked me how we were tracking our team leaders' coaching and how well they were doing it, which of course we haven't been doing."

"How well you do depends on your most junior and least-experienced managers' performance. If I were in your shoes, I would want to know what coaching they were doing and the quality of it," James added with a smile.

"You were insistent on that point," she agreed. "Now I understand why. We don't know what our team leaders and centre managers are doing. Let me show you how we measure performance."

She stood and fetched a sheet of paper from her desk. There was a diagram sketched on it.

Role

		Agents	Team leaders	Centre managers
Performance measures	Quantity	Sales made Conversion rate Calls completed Leads generated Call handling time Availability	◯	Adherence to budget
	Quality	Quality scores Sales retention Customer experience	◯	◯

Sally explained. "Most of our reporting shows the sales, service and productivity performance of our agents. Alongside the quantity measures, we judge the quality of sales by measuring the percentage retained for 90 days, and the quality of service by our customer experience measures. All our team and centre reporting is simply a combination of individual agent data."

Mark said, "We also check call quality. A quality team randomly listens to calls and scores them on pre-set criteria."

"You can see the problem we've got," said Jo-Anne. "We have no data on the quantity or quality of the coaching provided by our team leaders or centre managers. We're completely in the dark. We don't even know if poor and average performance is a problem with the agents involved, or with their team leaders."

Sally continued, "We've made our expectations clear on the coaching rhythm we want from our team leaders and centre managers. But we can't hold them accountable without visibility of what they're doing. If we can't see how our team leaders and centre managers are playing the game, we can't referee it. So I'm sure we won't be able to sustain the coaching culture we're creating, nor the performance gains we've made."

Mark was busy rolling up his shirt sleeves. He added, "I'm in full agreement. We're going to struggle without that visibility."

A coaching portal

"Top-performing team leaders do more coaching and are better at it than lower performers," James said. "So it would help if you had a coaching tracker – like a CRM or fitness tracker – for your team leaders to record all their coaching activity."

Sally laughed, glancing at the red band she wore on her wrist to track her daily steps. "Does such a thing even exist?"

"It certainly does," he replied. He stood and walked over to the window for a moment to stretch his back. Turning back to the group, James continued, "I'm involved with a company that's built an online coaching portal that has precisely this sort of functionality. Before I provide you with all the details, let's get clear on what you think you need in place to ensure there is consistent coaching across all your centres."

Mark said an online coaching tracker would be the perfect way to keep an up-to-date coaching record, making it simple for managers to record all their coaching activity and notes in one place. He'd then be able to see what his team leaders and centre managers were doing. With that information available to him, he could support them and hold them accountable for their coaching activity.

Jo-Anne nodded in agreement as she twirled a white stylus between her fingers. "That coaching tracker idea sounds like just the thing we need."

Sally got to her feet and walked over to a small whiteboard on the wall behind Mark. She took an eraser and wiped the board clean. Picking up a red marker, she began jotting notes.

She said, "A coaching tracker would be perfect for tracking coaching activity. But we also need a way to address coaching quality. Even if our managers spend more time coaching, it doesn't mean they're any good at it."

"HR runs an employee feedback survey from time to time. But it doesn't give us any insight into coaching quality," Jo-Anne commented. "We could regularly run a coaching survey to get that information. That would enable centre managers and team leaders to get periodic feedback from their team on what they're doing well with their coaching, and where they need to improve. From that data, we could create online action plans for them."

"Ideal," said Sally as she continued writing on the whiteboard. "Mark, you also mentioned we haven't yet trained our managers in all the High-Performance Coaching techniques. We would want to address that as well."

Mark thought the right approach might be to have the High-Performance Coaching content online. He mentioned he was a fan of micro-learning. He found that daily, bite-sized content delivered to his inbox helped him to quickly learn new concepts. Linking that content to short online videos on the coaching portal would allow managers to get more detail when they wanted it.

Jo-Anne added, "We'll also need to run initial coaching workshops to help our managers and team leaders to come up to speed with High-Performance Coaching. But once we've delivered them, the micro-learning idea

Mark mentioned would be a great way to keep the High-Performance Coaching practices top of mind."

Mark nodded in agreement. "Our training managers could run those workshops, provided they have access to lesson plans which take advantage of the online videos."

"Something that combined these elements would solve our problem," Sally declared. "James, does the coaching portal you spoke of provide what we are after?"

He smiled back, "Yes, it provides everything the three of you mentioned."

"What is it called?" enquired Jo-Anne.

"BravaTrak."

Mark raised his eyebrows. "BravaTrak?"

"I did say I was involved in the company that built it. So, I've had plenty of influence over its design," James replied with a shrug. "The BravaTrak coaching portal combines the components you mentioned: a coaching tracker, coaching survey, online action plans and daily micro-learning linked to a coaching course consisting of short video help guides.

"The company also supports centre managers and training managers to train team leaders in High-Performance Coaching and to implement the system. It's the only coaching portal I'm aware of developed specifically for contact centres. BravaTrak provides everything you need to create and sustain a world-class coaching culture, so you strengthen employee engagement and drive results."

Sally's notes

A Coaching Portal: how to referee the game

We have <u>no</u> visibility of the coaching activity of our managers and team leaders. We need to get this sorted if we are to create and sustain a world-class coaching culture.

We need:

- An online coaching tracker: for managers to record the coaching they've done.

- A coaching survey with online action plans: to get visibility of coaching quality.

- A coaching course with video content linked to daily micro-learning: to get managers trained in the High-Performance Coaching techniques.

The BravaTrak Coaching Portal seems like the answer. Check it out at www.bravatrak.com.

CHAPTER 15

END GAME

Mission accomplished

Sally leaned back in her office chair and stared out at the late-autumn day. The yachts in the harbour glowed in the sunshine. Today marked her ten-month anniversary with Velocity. More importantly, her division was more than meeting its sales, productivity and customer experience targets, exceeding them week after week. Now that she had control over the performance of her contact centres, all the stress she'd been experiencing had vanished.

To her great satisfaction, her home life had returned to normal as a result. Sally was able to spend time with her children in the morning and evening once again. And she and Michael had brought back their customary fortnightly date night. She felt she had restored the natural order of things.

Her relationship with Doyle had also been improving ever since she'd confronted him four months ago. Now he openly gave her credit for her recent achievements. He also listened to her point of view in a manner that suggested he was genuinely interested. She did feel a little guilty about this, knowing Trevor continued to struggle with performance in his retail network. He was almost certainly under even more pressure from Doyle because of her success. She'd told Trevor about the changes she was making, but he hadn't seemed interested.

None of this would have been possible without James and Alex – James for the guidance he'd provided and Alex for putting her in contact with him. In celebration, she'd taken them both out to Prego. It turned into a long lunch, and they'd managed to finish two bottles of wine between them. Sally had cleared her diary for the afternoon. She didn't expect to be doing much more work before an early departure.

She recalled her first meeting with James. It prompted her to look again at the creased sheet of paper on her desk, the sheet he'd given her with the High-Performance Coaching system diagram during their golf game months ago. She added some notes of her own, recording where the Coaching Portal components supported the High-Performance Coaching system.

The shift in performance had started when they'd understood what game they were playing and how they could win. It had accelerated when their team leaders and centre managers understood how to coach and when to coach. But it wasn't until her leadership team had visibility of what their managers were doing could they referee the game. That came about from putting the BravaTrak Coaching Portal in place. The reporting available had enabled Mark and Jo-Anne to identify those team leaders and centre managers who were coaching, and those who weren't. The results of the first coaching survey were also in. An interesting parallel had emerged. Team leaders who were consistently coaching had team members with higher employee engagement than those who weren't. Unexpectedly, unplanned leave had dropped across the centres, no doubt due to the improved engagement.

High-Performance Coaching system

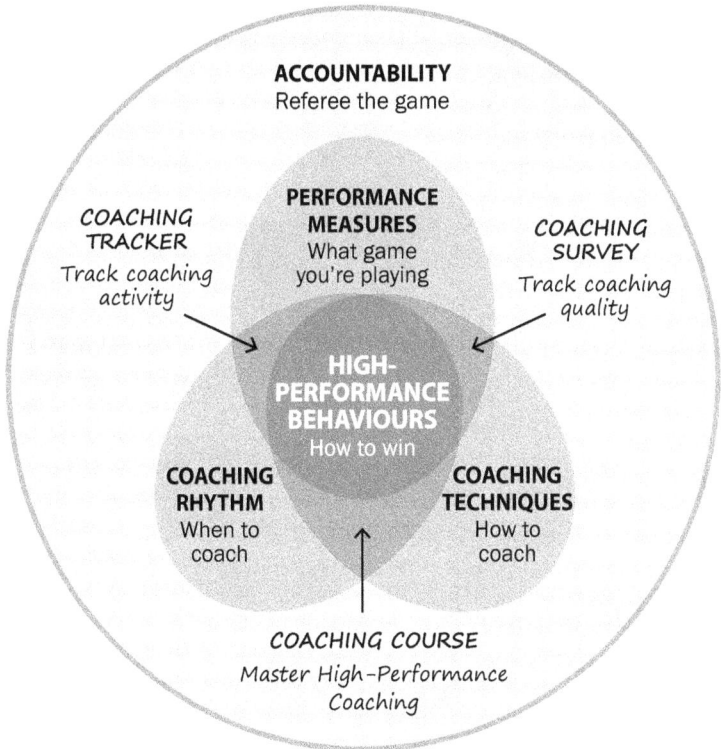

ACCOUNTABILITY
Referee the game

COACHING TRACKER
Track coaching activity

PERFORMANCE MEASURES
What game you're playing

COACHING SURVEY
Track coaching quality

HIGH-PERFORMANCE BEHAVIOURS
How to win

COACHING RHYTHM
When to coach

COACHING TECHNIQUES
How to coach

COACHING COURSE
Master High-Performance Coaching

Of course, this had led to some tough conversations with the centre managers and team leaders who'd been holding out. Sally had met with each of them one on one. She'd explained that High-Performance Coaching was how they now did business at Velocity, so they had a simple choice: either follow the system or leave the company. Then she had sat back and waited for their decision. The majority agreed to change, and for the most part, they had.

Sally laughed as she reflected on those conversations. *If only everything were so simple*, she thought. At that moment her phone rang. It was Doyle, asking if she had a minute to talk. Sally told him she'd be right there.

Bye-bye Trevor

On her way to his office, she passed Trevor in the corridor. His face was drained of colour, and his shoulders slumped. He carried a box filled with personal effects. To her surprise, he made no eye contact or comment as he went by.

When she reached Doyle's office, he stood and asked her to close the door. He gestured towards two comfortable chairs next to a low coffee table.

Doyle waited for Sally to take a seat before sitting down with his arms crossed. "I wanted you to be one of the first to know. Trevor has resigned to … spend more time with his family."

Sally cocked an eyebrow. She'd thought that Doyle had been overreacting to the board's pressure when he'd said their jobs were on the line, but it seemed he'd meant what he'd said.

Doyle ignored her look. "You've got a couple of good people in Jo-Anne and Mark. They can take care of the contact centre business by themselves for a while. I would like you to take over the retail network as acting General Manager while I find Trevor's replacement. It might take three to six months."

"But I don't have any retail branch experience," Sally protested, shifting in her chair. She felt terrible for Trevor, though they'd had little to do with each other outside of the senior leadership team meetings. Nor had he seemed interested in what she was doing to improve performance in her team.

"That's not necessary. You'll have an experienced team of regional managers, so they can guide you when needed. What they're missing is a robust coaching culture. I want you to put one in place. Are you up for the challenge?"

"I'm not going back to working fourteen-hour days."

"I don't expect you to. You've proven you've got what it takes. You know what to do, you have a great coaching system, and you have good people to delegate to. What do you say?"

Sally paused for a moment to consider. Perhaps she felt a little too relaxed from the wine at lunch, but she knew it was something she could achieve. After all, she now understood how to build a world-class coaching culture, and she had the technology to assist her with the BravaTrak Coaching Portal. The assignment would grow her reputation further as someone who delivered outstanding results.

She smiled and nodded. "Sure. I'll do it."

Game on, she thought.

How to find out more

To find out more about how a High-Performance Coaching system can help you create and sustain a world-class coaching culture, go to www.bravatrak.com

Claim your FREE Strategy Session at www.bravatrak.com/strategy

During your free, 45-minute video call with one of our experts, you'll get:

- An exact strategy to boost employee engagement and drive results using a High-Performance Coaching system.

- A gap analysis to identify the critical components missing in your current coaching approach.

- A risk factor analysis to determine the threats stopping you from building a coaching culture and getting the performance you want.

After the session, you'll receive a custom report with our recommendations on how to create and sustain a world-class coaching culture.

You may decide you need help with implementing this strategy. If so, and you're willing to follow our recommendations, we'll give you the opportunity for us to work together.

There will be no obligation to use our services.

Leave a review

If you found this book useful, we'd love you to leave a review. Just find the book's page on Amazon and then click on the button that says, "Write a customer review". We'd be very grateful – even if your review is just a line or two long.

Acknowledgements

Many people have contributed, in one way or another, to the development and success of our High-Performance Coaching system.

Mel Chandler – a friend, mentor and great coach – started me on the path. He taught me how to coach, and showed me that the techniques of sports coaching are just as effective at increasing performance at work.

Since then, numerous thought leaders have influenced my thinking. However, it's the people I've worked with who've helped me figure out what works best for our clients. In particular, I want to acknowledge Helen Jennings, Shelley Garden (nee Rushton), Anna Kingston and Mal Winnie for their contributions to our knowledge base, and their dedication to helping our clients succeed.

I've also learnt many lessons from our clients. I'm appreciative of the opportunity we've had to work with every single one of them.

Two people encouraged me more than any others to write this book: my wife, Gill White, and my son, Matt Stevenson. Gill has supported me through the good times and the bad, while Matt unexpectedly became my business partner a couple of years after he graduated from university. I'm deeply thankful for their love and support.

Matt wrote the first draft of this book by explaining our High-Performance Coaching system in story form. Although the story you read here has changed dramatically since that first draft, Matt gave me the gift of something to work with other than a blank page. I'm grateful beyond words for his help.

I'm also indebted to the following people who reviewed various drafts of the book: Graham Peters, Mark Burton-Brown and Helen Sao all gave me valuable feedback on early drafts. Martin Jennison corrected my descriptions of golf and soccer, and Jack Bauer provided me with the perspective of a professional athlete. Angela Wynn, Grant Joyes, Bridgette Dalzell, Suhail Shaikh and Sarah Mannion reviewed the later drafts. They helped ensure I addressed all their questions and provided guidance on how to make the story flow better.

Writing a business book in story form proved to be more challenging than I anticipated. I want to thank Suraya Dewing and Bruce Howat from The Story Mint for providing access to their unique online writing coach, Stylefit™, to assist me. If you found this story an engaging and easy read, it's because the Stylefit™ technology helped make it so.

Finally, I'd like to thank Michael Hanrahan and his team at Publish Central. They make self-publishing easy and stress free.

www.ingramcontent.com/pod-product-compliance
Lightning Source LLC
Chambersburg PA
CBHW061021220326
41597CB00017BB/2222